Writing Essay Exams
to Succeed
(Not Just to Survive)

Writing Essay Exams to Succeed
(Not Just to Survive)

SECOND EDITION

John C. Dernbach

Professor of Law
Widener University

ASPEN
PUBLISHERS

76 Ninth Avenue, New York, NY 10011
http://lawschool.aspenpublishers.com

© 2007 John C. Dernbach

Aspen Publishers
Attn: Permissions Department
76 Ninth Avenue, 7th Floor
New York, NY 10011-5201

Printed in the United States of America.

1 2 3 4 5 6 7 8 9 0

ISBN 0-7355-6282-2

Library of Congress Cataloging-in-Publication Data

Dernbach, John C., 1953-
 Writing essay exams to succeed (not just to survive) / John C. Dernbach. – 2nd ed.
  p. cm.
 Rev. ed. of: A practical guide to writing law school essay exams / John C. Dernbach. 2001.
 ISBN 0-7355-6282-2
 1. Law examinations–United States. 2. Legal composition. I. Dernbach, John C., 1953-Practical guide to writing law school eassay exams. II. Title.

 KF283.D47 2007
 808'.06634–dc22

2006019303

About Aspen Publishers

Aspen Publishers, headquartered in New York City, is a leading information provider for attorneys, business professionals, and law students.Written by preeminent authorities, our products consist of analytical and practical information covering both U.S. and international topics. We publish in the full range of formats, including updated manuals, books, periodicals, CDs, and online products.

Our proprietary content is complemented by 2,500 legal databases, containing over 11 million documents, available through our Loislaw division. Aspen Publishers also offers a wide range of topical legal and business databases linked to Loislaw's primary material. Our mission is to provide accurate, timely, and authoritative content in easily accessible formats, supported by unmatched customer care.

To order any Aspen Publishers title, go to *http://lawschool.aspenpublishers.com* or call 1-800-638-8437.

To reinstate your manual update service, call 1-800-638-8437.

For more information on Loislaw products, go to *www.loislaw.com* or call 1-800-364-2512.

For Customer Care issues, e-mail CustomerCare@aspenpublishers.com; call 1-800-234-1660; or fax 1-800-901-9075.

Aspen Publishers
a Wolters Kluwer business

FOR KATHY, BECKY, & TESS

SUMMARY OF CONTENTS

TABLE OF CONTENTS

6 ORGANIZATION, SIGNPOSTING, AND WRITING STYLE   53

7 GETTING READY   59

APPENDIX

PREFACE

If someone had told me, as a law student, that I would someday write a book on taking law school essay exams, I would have said nonsense, or something stronger. My objective then was to work in environmental law and make some contribution to the well-being of the planet, or at least my community. Exam writing — and teaching exam writing — seemed as far away from that as Jupiter.

Besides, the exam period was hardly my favorite time as a law student. I knew then, and still remember, the long hours of preparation, the stress of the exam itself, the irresistible but pointless urge to second-guess myself after the exam, and the thrill and agony of the grades that followed. Why would I want to revisit that, even in a different role?

But the kernel for this book came from my experience as a law student, because I learned more about exam taking from other students than from my professors — as brilliant and thoughtful as they were in the subjects they taught. Indeed, it sometimes seemed that my professors had a greater intuitive understanding of what they wanted than they were able to explain. The late professor Philip Kissam described exam-taking skill as "the knowledge of things 'we know but cannot say.'"[1] "Read the problem and then write like hell," one of my professors advised. That helped, but only a little. It also seemed that some students came to law school with a much greater understanding than others of how to answer essay exams. And I learned, as all law students do, that grades matter.

Most of my career thus far has, as it turned out, been anchored in environmental law, but I've also taught legal writing, mostly memos and briefs. When you teach writing, your grading has to focus a lot on writing itself. Much of the grade also hinges on analysis. But at day's end, as obvious as it sounds, writing is a core skill in a writing

---

[1] Philip C. Kissam, *Law School Examinations*, 42 Vand. L. Rev. 433, 460 (1989).

course. That has consequences for teaching, because students should be told in advance what good writing means and then graded according to those expectations.

When I started teaching doctrinal courses (a law professor name for courses in specific subjects, such as property or environmental law), I found myself focusing almost exclusively on the subject itself—the cases and statutes. We worked hard on that in class, and on hypothetical cases based on the material in the text. But something was missing. I wasn't telling students how to write answers to the essay exam that would come at the end of the semester. The omission seemed significant because the material in the course did not lead clearly and obviously to a particular way of answering essay exams. With the help of my experience teaching legal writing, the kernel of insight from my law student days started to germinate.

After talking to other law professors about what they expected in essay exams, and how they graded, I began experimenting with two-page handouts in my property and environmental law classes to explain the exam-writing process. Students told me they found these handouts helpful. Several years later I expanded these handouts to a 20-page handout. The longer handout was the precursor for this book. After they graduated, or had any reason to flatter me, former students told me it was helpful to them, even game-changing. After the first edition of this book was published, former students told me the same thing about the book itself. The book has enabled students to move from the bottom of the class to the middle of the class, or from the middle to the top. It has also helped law school graduates pass the bar exam and thus provide useful legal services to others.

This book borrows a good deal from my experience teaching legal writing to law students and from ideas contained in a textbook I coauthored.[2] Like the legal writing book, this volume demystifies the writing process in plain English, with a lot of examples and illustrations. This book also borrows from years of subsequent

---

[2]John C. Dernbach, Richard V. Singleton II, Cathleen S. Wharton, Joan M. Ruhtenberg, and Catherine J. Wasson, *A Practical Guide to Legal Writing and Legal Method* (3d ed., Aspen forthcoming 2007).

experience grading law school essay exams in property, administrative law, environmental law, and other courses. The process and the principles stated here are similar to what you will be taught, or have been taught, about writing legal memos and legal briefs. They also reflect a remarkable level of consensus among law professors about how essay exams should be written.

The many students who have found this guide helpful over the past several years, and who have told me so, led me to keep improving it. More than anyone else, they are responsible for this book. Ben Barros, Dennis Corgill, Brad Fogel, Charlie Geyh, Jim Krier, Christina Kunz, Kathy Nelson, Zyg Plater, Bob Power, and Elizabeth Samuels are among the many friends and colleagues who offered constructive and insightful suggestions on the manuscript for the first edition, this second edition, or both. Sheila Jarrett at Fred B. Rothman & Co. was instrumental in the publication of the first edition, and I have not, until now, publicly thanked her for that. For this edition, thanks also go to the legal writing and academic support faculty at Widener University Law School, especially Ann Fruth, Anna Hemingway, and Catherine Wasson, to Paula Heider and Kim Peterson for secretarial support, and to Robert Altenburg, Widener Class of 2008. Thanks, too, to the faculty and administration at St. Thomas University Law School in Miami, particularly Gordon Butler and Bob Butterworth. At Aspen Publishers, many thanks go to George Serafin, Carol McGeehan, Betsy Kenny, Kaesmene Harrison Banks, Iris Greidinger, and Jan Cocker. Any shortcomings, of course, are my responsibility.

INTRODUCTION

The opportunities that are available to you after law school, particularly in the years immediately following graduation, will depend on your grades. The better your grades are, the more likely you are to get the kind of job you want. This is generally true regardless of the kind of legal career you choose. Until you have been out of law school long enough to establish your credentials and skills by other means, prospective employers will use your grades as a measure — perhaps the key measure — of your ability. Your grades, in turn, will be based largely on your performance on essay exams. In addition, half of the bar exam in most states — the test that determines whether you can practice law — is an essay exam similar to that given in law schools. Whatever your previous experience, you almost certainly have not seen anything quite like a law school essay exam.

Students who do well in law school tend to write their exams in a particular way. The purpose of this short book is to introduce you to that method. It is short to keep you focused on the most important things you need to know. You may also find that this book will help you study more effectively day to day.

The basic object of an essay exam is problem solving. The reason is simple: Lawyers are problem solvers. People do not come to a lawyer because they want to hear a brilliant explanation of the law (although some would like that, too). People often come to lawyers for sympathy, but they want more than that. People come to lawyers when they are in trouble or something has gone wrong. They also come to lawyers when they want to make business deals or write a will. These are complex factual situations that present real problems to be solved.

For every problem a lawyer faces, he or she must learn the factual background of the problem, figure out the relevant legal rules, and determine how the law applies to the facts. Similarly, each essay problem in a law school exam will contain several paragraphs of factual information as well as a statement of the specific question or questions that need to be resolved. Students must figure out the correct legal rules and the relevant facts, and explain how the law leads to a particular conclusion.

Law school essay exams thus reflect, in important ways, the practice of law. They are intended to provide a basis for evaluating your ability to "think like a lawyer." Because thinking like a lawyer is perhaps the core skill taught in law school, it is not surprising that most students haven't seen this type of exam before law school.

A law school essay exam, of course, requires an extended written answer. That makes it different from an exam based on true/false, multiple choice, or short-answer questions. You may get some such questions on your exams in law school, but these are unlikely to form the basis for most of your grades. Having to write an extended answer means that you are not evaluated for what is in your head, what you would have written if it had occurred to you, or what you meant to say. Nor do you get credit for the things you don't write down because you think they're too obvious or because the professor already knows them. The professor wants to know what you know, and is not likely to assume, without evidence, that you know what you are doing. For better or worse, you are evaluated on what you actually write.

A law school essay exam is not like a standard undergraduate liberal arts essay exam. Although the word "essay" is used in both, it has a very different meaning in law school. Even when many undergraduate exams require essay answers, they are likely to ask what something means, why it exists, or what a particular writer had to say about it. The basic idea of many undergraduate exams is to find out whether you have absorbed the information provided in the course. A law school essay exam, by contrast, is intended to test your analytical ability in complex problem solving — to find out whether you can apply what you have learned to a specific problem. Thus, an undergraduate exam dealing with property rights might ask about the different approaches of Locke and Marx. An undergraduate pre-law exam might ask what the elements of a valid gift are and why we have these rules. By contrast, a law school exam will ask you whether, applying the law to a particular set of facts, there probably was a valid gift. You need to know what the rules are, but you also need to know how to apply that knowledge.

Perhaps surprisingly, a law school essay exam is in some ways like a mathematics or chemistry exam. Using formulas and equations learned in class, math and chemistry students are expected to solve specific problems. Also like law school essay exams, students in such exams are ordinarily not allowed to simply write down the answer; they must also show their work by writing the steps that led to the answer. Law school essay exams are nonetheless different from chemistry or math exams in at least two ways. First, the explanation on a law school exam must be in words, not in numbers or formulas. Second, law school essay exams do not ordinarily have a single correct answer. That's why it is particularly important to "show your work" — the steps of your analysis. In fact, your analysis is much more important than the conclusions you reach. You often need to scout out several lines of argument and possible answers, and explain steps you didn't take. Much of the time, you are simply predicting answers based on the facts. Whatever your background, then, you are likely to find law school essay exams unique.

Chapter 1 ("Your Reader") introduces you to the purpose of an essay exam and the general expectations of the professor who will grade it. Chapter 2 explains how your professor scores and grades your exam and provides an overview of how to do well. The process for getting started is described in Chapter 3 ("Beginning the Process"). Chapter 4 ("From Process to Writing") gives you a "big picture" overview of the basic steps in writing an essay exam. Chapter 5 ("Explaining Your Answer") builds on the previous chapter by providing detailed guidance on stating the law, applying the law to facts, and analyzing counterarguments. Basic organizational, signposting, and writing rules are described in Chapter 6. The last chapter, Chapter 7, provides overall guidance on how to get ready for essay exams. The text uses an exam problem to illustrate a variety of points. An appendix contains two additional exam problems, each of which is followed by several answers, including a model answer. Using the lessons in this book, the appendix troubleshoots the weaker answers and explains how to correct or avoid the errors they exemplify.

The real measure for the effectiveness of this book is whether it helps you write better essay exam answers. But simply reading it once will not likely be enough. A lot of guidance is packed into relatively few pages. Many students have found it helpful to study the sample answers or review sections of this book at least every semester. By rereading this book in light of their most recent exam-writing experience, in other words, they often see its guidance in a new light.

Of course, your professor is the final authority for how to write his or her essay exam. Law professors may provide a variety of different kinds of exam-taking help to their students, and some provide more guidance than others. Take this advice very seriously. Your professor, after all, is the one who will grade your exam.

Writing Essay Exams to Succeed
(Not Just to Survive)

YOUR READER

Your reader is the professor or instructor who teaches your class and who will prepare and then grade the exam or exams you will take. Your reader probably regards grading as the least pleasant part of his or her job. A colleague of mine says, "I would teach for free, but you have to pay me to grade." Still, the professor recognizes that grades matter a great deal to students and prospective employers, and tries to make sure that his or her grades are fair and accurate.

Purpose of Essay Exams

The exam is intended to test your knowledge of what the legal rules are. But, more importantly, it is also intended to test your ability to apply the legal rules to new factual situations. If you don't know the legal rules, the exam will be impossible, but your knowledge of the legal rules is only a starting point. It is possible to think you "know the law cold" and still do poorly on the exam. You need to be able to apply that law to specific factual situations; that's the most important part of the exam.

Most law school essay exams test two basic skills in applying the law to new factual situations. The first is determining what rule or rules are relevant to the question being asked. This is known as issue spotting. In any particular law school course, you will study a great number of rules; the first challenge of exam writing is to identify which of these rules *might* actually apply. If you write about the wrong rule, you are unlikely to get credit for your answer. Often, more than one rule *may be* applicable. It is thus important to be sure you have identified all of the relevant legal rules. The second skill in law school exams is applying these rules to the new factual situation stated in the problem. That is, you will analyze the rule(s) and explain how the rule(s) do or do not apply. Your analysis and explanation should be as complete and thorough as time allows.

The practical weight assigned to each of these skills will vary from professor to professor and may even vary year to year with the same professor. Some professors value issue spotting more than analysis and explanation, while others assign more weight to analysis and explanation. Some treat the two skills equally. The issues in some exams are relatively easy to identify, while relatively hard to identify in others. The "analysis and explanation" part of some exams is more straightforward than it is in others. Virtually all law school essay exams, however, focus to some degree on both of these skills.

These two skills have many analogues in the real world of law practice. When a client comes into your office, she wants you to be able to identify the legal rules that are relevant to her questions. She is not interested in how much law you know; she wants your help in resolving her particular problems. You can't do that unless you can figure out what legal rules are relevant to her situation. Similarly, when you make a closing statement to a jury in a trial, write a memo for a client, or write a brief to a court, your job is to analyze and explain in detail how a particular rule applies or does not apply to a specific factual situation. While essay exams do not test all of the skills you will need to practice law, they do test key skills.

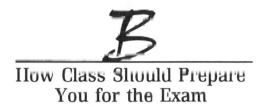

How Class Should Prepare You for the Exam

Your reader, the professor, prepares you for the exam from the first day of class. One of the subjects covered in a standard first-year property course, for instance, is land transfers — typically the sale of property by one party to another. Students learn that there are two major legal events in the purchase of land: signing the contract for sale of the property, and the closing, which normally occurs many weeks later. At the closing, the deed for the property is passed to the buyer, who then becomes the new owner.

A number of legal issues may arise concerning the contract. Each of those issues is normally covered in one or more of the cases that you have been assigned to read before class. In each of those cases, the court is applying legal rules to factual situations that are different from any that it had previously faced, and sometimes modifying those rules in the process. You should prepare a case brief for each of the cases you read for class. A case brief is a written summary of the case that includes the relevant rule(s), the facts, the issue(s) in the case, the court's holding(s), and the reasons and policies the court applied.

Before entering into a land contract, the seller has a duty to disclose material defects. Many property casebooks feature the famous New York case of *Stambovsky v. Ackley*,[1] in which the seller had created the public impression that the house being sold was haunted. She and her family told stories to national magazines

---

1. 572 N.Y.S.2d 672 (App. Div. 1991). Contrary to popular belief, this is not the case on which the book, *The Amityville Horror*, and the subsequent movie, were based. In that case, a man murdered his parents and four brothers and sisters in their home in Amityville, New York. When he was prosecuted, he claimed to have been possessed by demons. When the house was later sold, the seller and realtor told the buyers about the multiple murders that had taken place in the house, and reduced the price accordingly. The sellers then moved in, "allegedly experienced psychic phenomena traditionally associated with a 'haunted house'" for 28 days, and then moved out. They hired Jay Anson to write their story, which then sold 3 million copies and provided the basis for the movie. *See Lutz v. De Laurentiis*, 260 Cal. Rptr. 106, 107 (Ct. App. 1989).

and the local newspaper of seeing poltergeists in the house over the previous nine years. The seller said nothing about it before the contract was signed, and the buyer was unaware of the house's reputation. When the buyer found out, he wanted the contract rescinded. The Appellate Division of the New York Supreme Court agreed with the buyer and announced a new rule:

> *Where a condition which has been created by the seller materially impairs the value of the contract and is peculiarly within the knowledge of the seller or unlikely to be discovered by a prudent purchaser exercising due care with respect to the subject transaction, nondisclosure constitutes a basis for rescission as a matter of equity.*[2]

The major cases in the text are not the only things you should read. Often, there is explanatory or note material before or after the cases that provides additional detail on particular points, explains the history of the law, asks questions about hypothetical problems, and in other ways is intended to add to your understanding. Thus, the cases or notes in your text may distinguish two kinds of claims about material defects: objective and subjective. The objective test is whether the defect would be important to a reasonable person deciding to purchase the property. An objective defect might be a leaking roof or a cracked foundation; it would be hard to argue reasonably that such conditions are not material defects. The subjective or psychological test is whether the condition affects the value of the home to a particular buyer. A subjective defect might be the fact that someone was murdered in the house ten years ago; the murder doesn't affect the condition of the house, but some people wouldn't want to live in such a house and would be upset if they weren't told about it.

In class, the professor will ordinarily spend time making sure that the class understands the material. Then he or she will ask questions that force the class to think about factual situations not contained in the cases, or about issues that are mentioned only briefly in the text. For example, if the seller has AIDS, should he or she be required to disclose that? How is a house in which a person

---

2.   572 N.Y.S.2d at 676.

with AIDS lives similar to or different from a house with a reputation for being haunted? If disclosure is required, is that fair to people with AIDS?

The professor may also raise questions about the rules stated in the cases. The professor may explain that the *Stambovsky* rule is a reasonable statement of the law, with one possible exception. Let's take the *Stambovsky* facts, he or she might say, and make only one change. What if the seller of that house had done nothing to further the house's reputation as haunted, but had bought it from the person who did? Is the outcome here different? This forces students to think about the requirement, stated in the rule, that the seller creates the condition. If the seller knows of a material defect but doesn't disclose it, the professor may ask, should it matter that the seller didn't create it?[3]

Thus, the basic idea is not simply to memorize the rules. The professor is trying to get you to think about how the rules should apply to factual situations not directly answered by the material in your text. The professor is also trying to get you think critically about the rules themselves. The basic idea is to be able to apply the right rules, on your own, to new factual situations.

From Class to the Exam

When your professor prepares an essay exam, he or she will ask you to apply the rules you learned in class to another hypothetical problem. Because professors are obliged to assign grades, they write an exam that will enable them to make distinctions among various answers. If the exam is too easy, everyone will do well and it will be hard to make distinctions. If the exam is too hard, everyone will do poorly and, again, it will be hard to make distinctions. Thus, the exam ordinarily will contain a mix of relatively easy and

---

3. *See* John G. Sprankling, *Understanding Property Law* § 21.02[B][3][d] (2000).

relatively difficult parts. The following property exam problem is an example:

P R O B L E M

60 Minutes

Daniel Wallace owned a house in which Herman Melville lived for a year while he was writing *Moby Dick*. At Wallace's request, the house was included in promotional brochures for the city and several tour companies, as well as in several well-known travel books. The house was already mentioned in one travel book when Wallace moved into it. People frequently stood out in front of the house, looking at it and taking pictures. Wallace, a writer, worked at home and enjoyed greeting tourists and showing them the house.

Every prospective buyer was told that Melville had lived in the house for a year, including Amy Hayakawa. When Wallace got ready to sell the house, he used Melville's former residence in the house to ask a higher price for it. When Hayakawa signed a contract to purchase the house less than a week ago, she agreed to pay that price.

Earlier today, Hayakawa stopped by the house with a friend. To her horror, she discovered a busload of foreign tourists parked in front of the house, taking pictures and milling around on the yard and sidewalk. When she asked the tour bus driver what was going on, the driver said the tour company showed the house to tourists twice a month, and that Wallace often let them inside the house to look around.

Hayakawa has just come to you for advice. What are her legal options? What is her likelihood of success on each?

As you can see, this problem is similar in many ways to the *Stambovsky* case. In both cases, a buyer discovers something unpleasant about the house after signing a contract to purchase it. The problem here, of course, is not the same as the problem in *Stambovsky* or any of the problems discussed in class. Your job in answering this problem is to apply relevant legal rules to these facts.

Exam Preparation Requires Active Learning

Legal education is different in an important way from the kind of education many students have experienced earlier. Before law school, many students saw the teacher as active and themselves as passive: The teacher imparts information and they receive it; the teacher then tests for how well they have received it.

In legal education, both professors and students should be active, exchanging ideas, information, and perspectives. Students who are accustomed to being passive recipients of knowledge will find law school more challenging than those who are accustomed to active learning. In law school, the materials in the text apply only to a limited set of factual situations. While classroom discussion will apply that material to other situations, the exam will cover scenarios that you have never seen before. To prepare for this type of exam, you will need to be an active learner — briefing cases, preparing a course outline, doing additional reading when necessary, participating in study groups, working through hypothetical problems, and asking your professor questions.

Ultimately, getting ready for the exam is your responsibility. While your professor and friends or study group can help, only you will be writing the answer to your essay exam.

Outlining

As you move through a course, you should be writing a detailed outline. The outline is an essential study tool for the exam. When you prepare an outline, you pull together the most important material from the class, you organize that material, and you learn it better. Then, when you've prepared the outline, you study it in the same way that you would study published materials. You should be preparing your outline as you go through the semester. The material is much too dense and complicated to be mastered in the 24 to 48 hours before the exam.

The outline should include the basic rules from the cases as well as their underlying policies. If the rule has several elements, your outline should show those elements. You may want to include case names and key facts from those cases, but the outline should not be organized case by case. You may also want to include hypothetical problems discussed in class. In addition, your outline should include statutory or constitutional rules, as well as any cases that interpreted or applied the rules. Because your outline is a study tool, it must be accurate.

The simplest way to organize your outline for a course is to follow the organization of the text, as shown in its table of contents. The table of contents is divided into sections and includes major and minor headings. You should modify that outline for any changes contained in the syllabus provided by your professor. The professor may omit from his or her assignments some material contained in the text, or may add other material.

This outline should be your own work product, the result of your own thinking. A remarkable thing happens when you prepare an outline: You get a sense of how the pieces of the course fit together. By understanding the relationships among the parts, you better understand which rules might be applicable, and thus enhance your ability to spot issues and write about them.

SCORING
AND GRADING

What does your professor do with your exam after you turn it in? Contrary to what is often said, he or she does not throw exams down the stairs and award the best grades to those that land in a particular place — although it would be less time consuming to grade that way. Rather, your professor reads your answer and most will assign points to it. The highest grades go to the exams with the greatest number of points. Your job in answering an exam, then, is pretty straightforward: Score as many points as you can.

Scoring

Most professors use a grading system that assigns points to particular parts of an answer. They often work from a checklist of potential answers to generate a numerical score for each exam. The checklist system gives a professor a reliable means of measuring achievement (or lack of achievement) on the exam. A checklist helps ensure consistency from day to day in scoring. No professor wants to tell a student that she would have done better if he had read her exam Friday, rather than Monday, because he was in a better mood later in the week. A checklist also helps the professor review your exam for a variety of things.[1]

Virtually all of the time your professor spends with your exam will be in scoring — determining the number of points that your exam deserves. What distinguishes exams with higher scores from those with lower scores?

- In a problem that involves the applicability of two rules, exams with the highest scores will discuss both rules. Exams that miss one or, worse yet, both of these rules will score lower.
- In a problem that involves a three-element rule or a rule that raises three issues, exams with the highest scores will discuss all three elements or issues. Exams that discuss fewer elements or issues will score lower.
- In analyzing a single element or issue, exams with the highest scores will discuss as many relevant facts as possible, will identify and answer counterarguments, and will raise policy arguments in support of (or in opposition to) their conclusions. Exams with lower scores will mention fewer facts, even though more facts could be discussed; they will not raise counterarguments, and they will not raise policy arguments.

---

1.   Those professors who do not use a scoring system tend to look for the same things as those who do. They say, in effect, that they use a mental checklist instead of a written checklist while they read essay exams. Thus, the advice provided here can also be applied to those professors.

To summarize, there is a continuum on scoring, and it can be depicted like this:

The Scoring Continuum				
	Lowest Scores ←——		**——→ Highest Scores**	
Relevant Rules	None	One	Most	All
Relevant Elements/ Issues	None	Few	Most	All
Analysis of Each Element/ Issue	No Facts	Few	Most	All
	No Counter- arguments	Occasional Counterarguments	Many Counterarguments	
	No Policies	Occasional Use of Policies	Many Policies	
Conclusions	None	Few	Most	All

This continuum, however, does not tell the full story. Identification of the relevant issues, and the relevant elements for each issue, provides a foundation for writing your answer. If you don't do that, you may not score any points at all. But simply stating the rules, without more, will not get you very many points. Nor will drawing conclusions. The greatest opportunity to score points is in your analysis of each element. Thus:

Few Potential Points	**Many Potential Points**
Relevant Rules	Analysis of Each Element/Issue:
Relevant Elements/Issues	
Conclusions	— Facts
	— Counterarguments
	— Policies

B
Grading

Once your professor has finished scoring all of the exams, and placed the scores on a curve, he or she is almost finished. All scores are placed on a chart that enables the professor to see the high and low scores, as well as the overall distribution of scores. From that chart, the professor determines the letter or numerical grade that each exam will receive. Of course, the highest scores get the highest grades, and vice versa.

An actual curve from a recent class is on the facing page. Different professors will award different numbers of points than those shown here, but the shape of the curve and the distribution of scores is within the range of what we ordinarily see.

As you can see, the high score was 153 and the low score was 37. The median score is also an important score for professors. As you may know, a median score is not the average score. Rather, a median (88 for this exam) indicates that half the class scored more than 88 points, and half the class scored less than 88 points. Knowing the boundary line between the top half of the class and the bottom half of the class is extremely useful for grading.

Once the exams are scored, assigning a letter grade is pretty straightforward. As you might guess from the scoring curve shown above, teachers will tend to look for clumps of scores, and draw grading lines between the clumps. There is some degree of judgment in deciding where to draw those lines. But your overall score, more than anything else, determines your grade.

Most law schools have some kind of standard grading curve, also known as a grade normalization policy. The idea is to make sure that overall grades are relatively consistent from class to class, and from professor to professor. Most law schools do not want situations where the students in one class generally get A's, and the students in another class generally get C's or worse. We all know that some professors are "tougher" graders than others. We all know that some classes are harder than others. But a standard curve or normalization

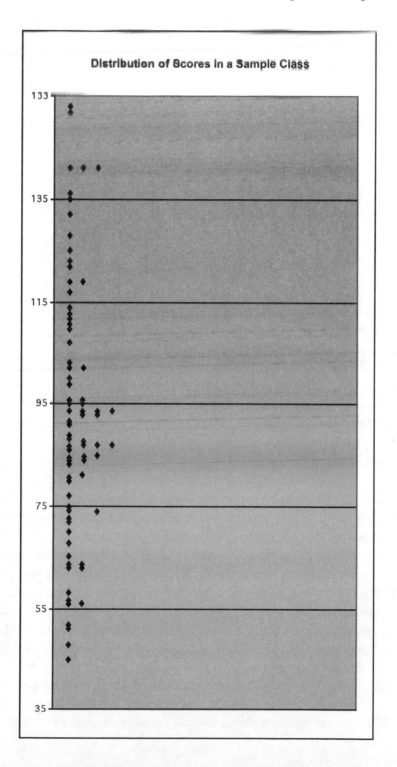

policy ordinarily prevents great disparities between the grades in the harder classes and the tougher professors, on one hand, and the grades in other classes and with other professors, on the other. Disparities often occur anyway, but they are not as large as they would otherwise be.

Whatever the grading curve or normalization policy at a particular school, students who score more points will get better grades than those who score fewer points. For students who are not satisfied with their grades, the trouble is not the curve. The trouble is that they are not scoring as many points as they should.

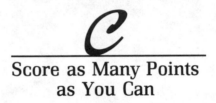

Score as Many Points as You Can

Your job, then, is to score as many points as you possibly can. Do not worry about how other students are doing. The only thing you can control is how many points you score. There is no such thing as a "perfect" answer to a law school essay exam. Some answers just earn more points than others.

This objective — scoring as many points as you can — is also very practical. Undergraduate students often receive a decent grade for a modest level of effort. When they come to law school, they may expect things to work the same way. That is a big mistake, because law school is much harder and more competitive than most undergraduate programs. It is not enough to work harder; you also must work smarter. (See Chapter 7.) Modest effort will most likely get you low grades, not decent grades. That's one of the reasons — though certainly not the only reason — that some law students receive lower grades than they did as undergraduates. And if you write about the wrong issues on your exam, or can't analyze the problems, your grades could be far worse.

Students are often disappointed with their first-semester or first-year grades. Sometimes, they respond by scaling back their level of effort or seeing themselves as less capable than their classmates.

That's also a mistake. For starters, students tend to get higher grades in their later years of law school because they gain experience in taking exams, they better understand what is expected of them, and they study more effectively. Improvement in grades is often dramatic. Conversely, students sometimes work hard in their first year, receive very good grades, and then coast. It is easy for your grades to fall if you do that. Students whose grades go down after the first year — regardless of how well they did first year — are also at a higher risk of failing the bar exam.

One final thing: It is impossible to score as many points as you can unless you are really motivated to do well. Some students know exactly what they want from law school, and what they plan to do with their law degree, but some students are ambivalent or uncertain about their goals. For the first group, motivation usually is not a concern. Those of us who teach law see classrooms full of talented students. The admissions process at law schools ensures that our students have considerable achievement and potential before they step into the classroom. What usually separates the high achievers from the others, though, is not how much raw talent they have. What separates the high achievers — in law school and in the real world of law practice — is their motivation.

Virtually everyone comes to law school with experience in some activity or endeavor that engaged — or perhaps still engages — him or her at a high level of intensity. This other activity may involve sports, academic work, theater, nature, cooking, or anything else. The challenge — if you want to do as well as you can — is to apply at least that level of intensity to class preparation and answering essay exams. I have reviewed final exams with a great many students over the years, and of course many are unhappy with their grade. Just about everyone, though, has had some experience from high school or college (often playing sports) that has really charged his or her batteries. "Did you practice hard?," I ask. "Of course," they say. "Did you play to win?," I ask. "You bet," they say, a little surprised at the apparent stupidity of the question, but often willing to share favorite memories. "Do you approach your law studies that way?," I ask. All too often, after a long pause, the answer is no. They have never even considered the possibility of applying that same level of intensity to their study of law. I made that point to the first-year class at another law school recently and was approached afterwards by a student who introduced himself as an Olympic bronze medalist. He certainly looked the part. It had never occurred to him, he said, to apply to law his intense approach to Olympic training. He had been treating his studies as just another thing he had to do, and that, he added, was going to change.

Not everyone wins an Olympic medal, even those who try their hardest, and not everyone graduates at the top of his or her class at law school. But trying your hardest will likely get you better results than if you don't. Even if you are not sure what you want to do with a law degree, higher grades will give you more and better career choices after law school. Almost certainly, some students will do better than you and some will do worse. Whatever your feelings about your classmates, you can't control how well they score. What matters, and what you can control, is how well you do. Do your best, and let the curve fall where it may.

The Tao of Knowing Law
for Essay Exams

Students who are unhappy with their grades often say that they "know" the law and that the grade does not reflect what they "know." But there are many levels of knowledge in law. Which do you think is tested on essay exams?

(A) I know it because I can recognize it.
(B) I know it because I memorized it.
(C) I know it because I can explain how the cases applied it.
(D) I know it because I can apply it to new and different factual situations.

Answer A is a fairly typical answer for material that is tested on undergraduate multiple choice exams. Answer B captures what is often tested on college essay exams. Answer C would be right if your required learning were limited to mastering the cases in the text. Answer D is what is required in essay exams. Answers A, B, and C are all necessary skills, but only Answer D will make you a lawyer.

BEGINNING
THE PROCESS

The initial steps in the exam-writing process involve time allocation and issue spotting. You can begin the first even before you have read the problem.

Time Allocation

Law school essay exams tend to run from two to four hours, depending on the number of credits in the course. Each exam, in turn, is usually divided into several parts. A three-hour exam, for example, might contain three separate parts. Sometimes the parts are divided evenly, but sometimes they are not. The three-hour exam, for example, might contain a problem that counts for half the grade and two other problems that each count for a quarter of the grade. This method of dividing the exam has two important consequences for managing your time.

1. Allocate your time according to the value of the problem

When time suggestions are provided by the exam (e.g., 45 minutes for Problem I), follow them. If you are told in a three-hour exam that one problem will count for half the grade, use half the time (90 minutes) to answer it.

2. Treat each part as a separate exam

Write on one problem until your time is up or until you have nothing more to say. Even if you have more to say, wrap things up when the allocated time is over. Then write on the next problem, and so forth. Don't worry about whether your answer is perfect before you move on; every additional minute you take on this problem is a minute you don't have for the next one, and you are not likely to get as many points fine-tuning your first answer as you will get for writing the next one.

Some students figure that a three- or four-hour exam gives them a while to decide which problem to answer first. Some students find value in reading the entire exam and then deciding which problem they want to write about first; they might be more comfortable writing about some issues than others. But unless you have strong reason to think that might help you, you should simply move methodically from one problem to the next. Every minute you spend deciding which problem to answer first is a minute you are not using to answer any problem.

Issue Spotting

One of the key skills that professors test is your ability to identify the legal rules that are relevant to a particular problem: This is issue spotting. An issue exists if a plausible argument can be made that a relevant legal rule applies to the facts of that problem, or if the answer on that rule could "go either way" under the facts. It is not necessary that the rule ultimately be applicable. The rule must also be relevant; it must respond to the question.

Issue spotting requires you to understand both the question being asked and the legal rules covered in the course. Issue spotting is not simply an exam-taking skill. It is also a crucial part of law practice. When your client explains a problem to you, for example, you need to pay attention to what the client wants (the question being asked) and the factual situation, and you need to know the legal rules relevant to that problem. A hallmark of good lawyers is their ability to spot issues of importance to their clients.

Before you start writing, be sure to understand the question, understand the context, and identify the basic legal rules that could plausibly be used to address the problem.

1. Understand the question

The question or "call of the question" is what you are asked to do. Ordinarily, the question is contained at the end of the fact pattern or story in the problem. You may be asked to write an opinion based on these facts, to predict how a court would decide the case, to make the best arguments for one side, or something else. In the Hayakawa problem, the call of the question is to assess her options and assess the likelihood of success on each.

Law professors all too often read exam answers that have been based on misunderstandings of the question. Sometimes it's not even clear from the answer that the student read the question. Don't let the stress of the exam get in the way of your ability to make sense of the question. From a scoring perspective, the consequences of a mistake in understanding the question are great. For example, if you write about strict liability when the question asks about negligence, you may get no points at all for your answer.

Understanding the question is the most basic prerequisite for issue spotting. If you do not understand the question, you are not likely to identify the right issues. The factual situation contained in most essay exams usually covers a great many legal rules you studied in class. Use the question to focus on the legal rules that are relevant. Highlight or underline the question. Periodically check your answer-in-progress against it.

Some students find it helpful to read the call of the question first and then read the factual material on which the question based. By reading the question first, they have developed a sense of the relevant parts of the problem. If you do that, read the question again after you have read the rest of the problem.

2. Understand the context

Each problem in an essay exam comes with a story and characters, and you need to understand both. Sometimes, the story is complicated enough that you need to diagram it or draw a picture. This often happens in property exams where there are multiple transactions or where the description of a parcel doesn't convey as much information as the map you draw in your notes. While you don't know very much about the characters, you do know what happens to them in the story and you should have a pretty good idea from the story what they want. The characters in the story are usually litigants or potential litigants. Often, in the story, they make statements or act in ways that reveal their objectives. Think of them as genuine people, and figure out what they care about. This is, by the way, exactly what lawyers do in the real world.

Essay exam problems typically involve parties who are making opposing claims or who are opposing each other in litigation. In essay exams and in real life, if there is a lawsuit, you can be very sure that the defendant will explore every possible way of resisting liability, including affirmative defenses. If a claim is based on one interpretation of facts, you can also be sure that the person against whom the claim is made will see if the facts can be interpreted differently or if there are other facts that support her position. The better you understand each of the characters in the story, the more likely you are to see counterarguments. Counterarguments are arguments, often based on relevant facts and policies not already discussed, for a conclusion opposing the one you reach. Sometimes there is no plausible defense to a lawsuit or no possible answer to a claim. But you are not likely to see an essay exam based on such cases and, in any event, that conclusion should be reached only after careful analysis.

Understanding the context is essential to issue spotting because it helps you understand what legal rules could be invoked on behalf of the characters in the story, and what legal rules will likely be invoked in response. It also helps you understand what facts will be important to each person who has a stake in the legal outcome. And it will help you evaluate possible remedies.

3. Identify the basic legal rules that could plausibly be used to answer the question

To a great degree, issue spotting involves pattern recognition. In preparing an essay exam, a professor will ordinarily develop fact patterns that are similar to, but not the same as, the cases you read for class. When you read the problem, you should see those similarities. The better you know those cases, the more likely you are to spot relevant issues.

Some questions involve only one relevant rule, so your identification of the rules will be complete when you find that one. Other questions (in fact, most questions) will involve more than one relevant rule. Therefore, don't quit looking for relevant rules after you have found one. Make sure you have found all of the relevant rules, realizing that some issues will likely be easier to spot than others. When more than one question is asked, moreover, be sure you are responding to each question.

Students who find and discuss two or more relevant rules tend to do far better on essay exams than those who find and discuss only one. Consider two students, Maria and Louise, who both see the same issue in an essay problem and write about it equally well. Maria, however, sees a second issue and writes an answer to that issue that is as long and effective as her answer on the first issue. Maria is likely to get twice as many points for her answer to this problem as Louise, and will likely get a much higher grade.

Sometimes a problem raises more than one issue, but the resolution of the first issue in a particular way may seem to make discussion of the other issues unnecessary. A problem might involve a lawsuit against your client, and the question requires an assessment of your client's potential liability and the remedies (e.g., damages, injunctive relief), if any, to which she is most vulnerable. You may conclude that your client is not liable and therefore not subject to any remedies. But if you don't discuss remedies, you are making a big mistake. There will probably be grounds for a different conclusion, or your conclusion might be wrong. Either way, you need to write about the remedies that a court might order against your client. You can begin your answer to this part of the question by saying something like this: "If, despite the previous analysis, she is held liable . . . "

In developing your answer, everything that was in your assigned reading or covered in class is fair game — regardless of how easy or hard it seems. Unless you are told otherwise, you should not consider other material in your answer, or worry about studying it.

For each essay problem, write an issues checklist before you begin your answer. The checklist doesn't need to be any more than some shorthand references to each relevant rule. This becomes the basic outline for your answer. The checklist also becomes a kind of navigational device; when you are through writing about the first issue, your checklist will show you the next thing you need to write about.

Students often think that they need to start writing right away, and having a few sentences written almost immediately may give you a sense of security or confidence. If you don't have a plan (and a good one), however, you are likely to repeat yourself, concentrate on one issue to the exclusion of others, and even write about the wrong issues. You may even find yourself crossing out several pages of your answer and starting over midway through the allotted time. Think before you write.

If you find that you can't think of any relevant legal rules for a particular problem, you might consider setting that problem aside and reading the next problem, which may be easier. Coming back to the previous problem, you may have thought of the relevant issues. This is not something you should plan to do, however; it is a damage-control strategy for that rare situation when you simply find yourself stuck.

To get a sense of how these principles work, let's revisit the essay problem from Chapter 1.

PROBLEM

60 Minutes

Daniel Wallace owned a house in which Herman Melville lived for a year while he was writing *Moby Dick*. At Wallace's request, the house was included in promotional brochures for the city and several tour companies, as well as in several well-known travel books. The house was already mentioned in one travel book when Wallace moved into it. People frequently stood out in front of the house, looking at it and taking pictures. Wallace, a writer, worked at home and enjoyed greeting tourists and showing them the house.

Every prospective buyer was told that Melville had lived in the house for a year, including Amy Hayakawa. When Wallace got ready to sell the house, he used Melville's former residence in the house to ask a higher price for it. When Hayakawa signed a contract to purchase the house less than a week ago, she agreed to pay that price.

Earlier today, Hayakawa stopped by the house with a friend. To her horror, she discovered a busload of foreign tourists parked in front of the house, taking pictures and milling around on the yard and sidewalk. When she asked the tour bus driver what was going on, the driver said the tour company showed the house to tourists twice a month, and that Wallace often let them inside the house to look around.

Hayakawa has just come to you for advice. What are her legal options? What is her likelihood of success on each?

As you can see from the description at the beginning of the problem (Problem 1 (60 minutes)), you would have 60 minutes to answer this problem. The time starts when you begin reading the problem and ends one hour later, whether you have finished writing your answer or not.

There are two questions here: identification of Hayakawa's legal options and her likelihood of success on each. Because the Hayakawa problem does not name any particular rule, you need to figure out the rule(s) from clues provided. One important clue here is that Hayakawa signed the contract less than a week ago.

Another is that she discovered an apparent difficulty with the house after she signed the contract. (You also have the clues provided by the *Stambovsky v. Ackley* case in Chapter 1!) This exam problem thus involves land transfers, which should take you to the part of the course concerning contracts to purchase real estate, and particularly the duty to disclose defects. Failure to disclose material defects, as we saw earlier, is grounds for rescission of the contract. Although not discussed in Chapter 1, fraudulent misrepresentation of a material defect is also grounds for rescission.

These are both arguable grounds for rescission of the contract in this problem. Wallace was not asked about the tourists, and never said anything to Hayakawa, which could fit the failure-to-disclose rule. There could also be misrepresentation here, albeit indirectly. By emphasizing that Melville's residence in the house made it more attractive, Wallace arguably was saying there was nothing to worry about.

The problem raises at least one more legal option. She could go ahead with the deal and then use the trespass rule to prevent tourists from walking on the property. In general, trespass is any intentional and unprivileged entry onto land owned or occupied by another. The most common remedies for trespass are injunctive relief and damages. In order to take advantage of these remedies, though, she would first need to own the property. Because she has only signed a contract, and has not obtained the deed for the property, she is not yet the owner.

As for the second question — likelihood of success on each option — you probably won't have a good answer to that until you have actually analyzed the options. Because Hayakawa is your client, you have a professional obligation to tell her the truth about her likelihood of success, whether she wants to hear it or not. Be aware as you start writing that Wallace has some strong counterarguments; the fact that a famous author once lived in the house, for instance, is not ordinarily considered a negative thing. Hayakawa also had far more knowledge about the notoriety of the house than did the buyer in *Stambovsky*. How much of that notoriety wasn't disclosed adequately to the buyer? Was that nondisclosure fraudulent? So you should keep yourself focused on both arguments and counterarguments as you write your answer.

Thus, an issues outline for your answer to this problem might look like this:

Assess Hayakawa's likelihood of success —

Failure to disclose
Fraudulent misrepresentation
Trespass

You should have this, or something like it, written in your notes before you begin to write your answer in any essay exam. You can even use the points in the outline as underlined headings when you write your answer. If you are required to discuss the legal rights or interests of multiple parties, be sure you have included each of these parties in your issues outline, along with a brief statement of the legal rules that are relevant to each. That will help ensure that you actually discuss the legal rights or interests of each party when you are writing your answer. Be sure, in sum, that your issues outline is fully responsive to the call of the question.

Handwriting vs. Typing

Many schools now offer students the option of answering their exam on a laptop computer instead of handwriting the exam. If you have this option, you should consider it seriously.

When I was in law school, we were given the opportunity to type our exam answers instead of writing them by hand. This was before personal computers were available, and I used a portable electric typewriter. I typed much faster than I could write by hand. In addition, my handwriting was hard to read when I wrote under pressure. So the typewriter enabled me to write more, and more legibly, than I could otherwise.

Laptop computers present a different situation from typewriters because they come with hard drives that can store lots of information. To prevent students from cheating by using information stored on their hard drives, some companies have developed software programs for exam taking that block access to the hard drive during the exam period. These programs enable students to use a laptop in much the same way that I used my typewriter.

If you have the choice, and if you are comfortable with a laptop and type fairly fast, you should consider typing your exam. When, despite your best efforts, you need to insert text or move blocks of text, using a laptop can be handy. If your handwriting under pressure borders on illegible, you should also consider typing. Otherwise, do what seems comfortable and appropriate. Typing does not make you more knowledgeable or better prepared, however. Not does it assure you of a higher grade.

FROM
PROCESS
TO WRITING

Spotting the right issues is a huge first step, but it is only that. For each relevant rule, your answer needs to do three things: identify each element of the rule, apply each element to the relevant facts, and draw a conclusion for each element and each rule.

The standard law school formula for solving legal problems is known as IRAC, an acronym for Issue, Rule, Application, and Conclusion. As you can see, the "I" part of IRAC is reflected in the previous chapter. The "RAC" part is described here.

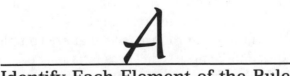

Identify Each Element of the Rule

To analyze a rule completely, you need to break the rule into elements and discuss each element separately. Once you've found the legal rule(s), identifying the elements should be straightforward. Many common law rules are based on lists of elements that are numbered for your convenience. Other common law rules, and most statutory rules, are based on elements that you can understand only if you break a sentence or sentences into parts. This is true of the rule in Problem 1. As part of your outline of the course work, you should already have broken such rules into elements.

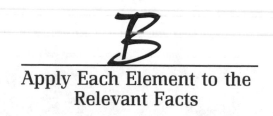

Apply Each Element to the Relevant Facts

When you apply a legal element to facts, you are really doing two things: You are describing facts that are legally relevant, and you are explaining how these facts lead to your conclusion. Once you have identified each element, find facts in the problem that correspond to it. Use as many facts from the problem as you can, including facts that tend to undermine your tentative conclusions about how the question should be answered. Reading and rereading the problem helps you identify those facts. If you find "unnecessary" facts in the question, there is also a very good chance that they raise another issue or suggest a counterargument to an existing issue.

Before starting to write, some students highlight, underline, or otherwise mark those facts. Some simply take mental note of particular facts, though they risk forgetting them in the rush of writing their answer. Others reread the problem as they write about each element, looking for relevant facts.

Professors will often introduce facts that are completely irrelevant to the question being asked. These facts may even suggest the importance of rules that are, in reality, unrelated to the question. Professors include these "red herrings" because irrelevant facts and law come up all the time in law practice. Clients often tell their stories without knowing what matters, and you need to be able to recognize when facts are not relevant.

Identifying the relevant facts is a good start, but in many situations, the facts themselves do not lead unquestionably to one particular conclusion. When that occurs, you need to explain why the facts lead to your conclusion. All too often, law students think that applying the law to the facts simply means identifying the facts that correspond to specific elements, and then drawing a conclusion without further discussion. Sometimes the rule is so precise and the facts so clear that little explanation is required. But most of those cases are resolved without lawyers, and are unlikely to find their way onto your exam.

C

Write a Conclusion for Each Element and for Each Rule

As you write about a particular element, you will need to think about what your conclusion will be. In addition, you need to draw a conclusion for each overall rule, which, of course, will be based on your conclusions for each element. Be sure to state these conclusions clearly in your answer. Much of the time, your conclusion will simply be a prediction of how a court would likely decide the particular issue. If there is little doubt about the outcome, your conclusion can be more definite. If there is a reasonable basis for more than one conclusion, then qualify your conclusion with words like "likely" or "probably." Remember that your conclusions are much less important than your analysis.

Some law school essay exams will ask you to advocate a particular position on behalf of a client, in much the same manner as a lawyer would represent a client in real life. In such exams, of course, the basic conclusion is already established before you begin writing, but everything else should be the same as for an exam in which you are asked to reach your own conclusions. Similarly, some professors simply want you to describe arguments and counterarguments, and are not interested in your conclusions. In that case, of course, you can simply skip conclusions.

A student's answer to the Hayakawa problem might look like Answer 1. Let's focus on the failure-to-disclose issue to keep the example manageable:

A N S W E R

Hayakawa recently signed a contract to purchase property and then discovered a problem. She wants to know her legal options and her likelihood of success for each.

Failure to disclose. Hayakawa's first option is to rescind the contract, if she can show that Wallace failed to disclose a material defect. Where the seller creates a condition that materially impairs the value of a contract, and is peculiarly within the seller's knowledge or is unlikely to be discovered by a prudent buyer exercising reasonable care, nondisclosure is a basis for rescission.

First, the condition is that a large number of tourists visit the house, including at least two busloads per month. They stand outside on the sidewalk and in the yard, taking pictures and expecting to come inside.

Second, Wallace, the seller, created the condition because he requested that the house be used in promotional brochures for the city and several tour companies, as well as in several well-known travel books. It appears that his promotional effort is the reason that a tour company bus stops in front of his house twice a month. Wallace might say the house was already in one travel book when he moved into it. But now, because of his efforts, it is in several brochures and travel books. Wallace might also say he is not responsible for the fact that Melville lived in the house for a year. That is true, but he is responsible for the increase in tourists, which is the relevant condition. Besides, if all the other elements are met, a court might decide it doesn't matter whether he created the condition. As a matter of equity or fairness, if Wallace failed to disclose a condition of which Hayakawa could not reasonably be aware, Wallace should not profit from his behavior.

Third, is this condition a material defect? There are two possible tests for a material defect. The objective test for a material defect is based on whether a reasonable person would attach value to the defect in deciding whether to buy. A reasonable buyer would expect that the house would be more attractive because it is Melville's former residence, not less attractive. Indeed, Wallace asked — and received from Hayakawa — a higher price for the house because it is Melville's previous residence. A reasonable person would buy a home for a residence, and would expect privacy in his or her home. A reasonable person would probably recognize that some tourists may want to visit a former Melville home, but the same person would not likely buy a significant tourist attraction for use as a residence.

The routine presence of tourist buses and tourists, taking pictures and perhaps expecting a tour of the house interior, is not compatible with the privacy a reasonable person would expect in his or her home. Wallace might say the tour buses come only twice a month. But there are almost certainly tourists at other times, and the buses could become more frequent in the future. This condition is probably an objective material defect.

The subjective test is whether the condition affects the value of the home to the particular buyer. Hayakawa was horrified to find a busload of tourists outside the house. On that basis, the subjective test is probably met. It can be argued that she is a hypersensitive buyer, and that someone's feelings should not be grounds for rescission. If the buyer's feelings were enough, anyone could rescind a contract under the subjective test. Here, though, her negative reaction to the regular presence of tourists by the busload outside her home would probably be shared by a great many other people. That suggests she is not a hypersensitive buyer, and that there is some reasonable basis for her feelings.

Fourth, is the condition peculiarly within the seller's knowledge? Both Wallace and Hayakawa knew that Melville had lived in the house. But Wallace also knew the number of tourists and their expectation of coming inside the house, which Hayakawa didn't know. Therefore, the condition was peculiarly within Wallace's knowledge.

Fifth, was the condition unlikely to be discovered by a prudent buyer exercising reasonable care? She could have visited the house beforehand more often. Because the tourist buses come only twice a month at present, she might not have seen anything anyway. She could have perhaps found the passage in the travel books and brochures describing the house, but prudent buyers should not be expected to check such materials when buying a home. Also, she could not be expected to know everything that Wallace had done to promote Melville's former presence in the house.

On the other hand, she had to know that other people would also be interested in seeing the house where a famous author lived. A prudent buyer exercising reasonable care in the purchase of such a home should have asked Wallace about the possibility of tourists or other interested persons, but she didn't. Hayakawa is not likely to be able to satisfy this element.

Sixth, there was nondisclosure. It does not appear from the problem that Wallace said anything about tourists. He did use Melville's former residence in the house to get a higher price, and thus disclosed that a famous author had lived there. But a place where Melville lived for only one year is not automatically a significant tourist attraction.

Therefore, Hayakawa is probably not entitled to rescission of the contract based on nondisclosure of a material defect.

Fraudulent misrepresentation. A second option is to seek rescission based on fraudulent misrepresentation of a material defect. [Discussion omitted.]

Trespass. The third option is to complete purchase of the property and then use trespass to keep tourists away. [Discussion omitted.]

This answer has a structure that directly follows the principles stated in this chapter and the preceding chapter. It states the overall rule and works through the rule element by element. For each element, the answer states the element, describes the relevant facts, shows how the rule does or does not apply to these facts, and states a conclusion either at the beginning or the end of the discussion. At the end of the analysis, the answer includes a conclusion on the overall rule. The pattern would be repeated for the answers to the second and third rules, which are not shown here.

Exam Quest: A Mental Map

The pattern shown for answering this problem is the same in most essay exams. This pattern, or mental map, will help you understand exactly how your exam should be organized. It also gives you directions, at each step in writing your answer, for the next step you should take. The answer to a two-issue exam problem, when the first rule has two elements and the second rule has three elements, could be diagrammed like this:

RULE I

    Element 1
        Apply Element 1 to facts
        Conclusion on Element 1

    Element 2
        Apply Element 2 to facts
        Conclusion on Element 2

    Conclusion on Rule I

RULE II

    Element 1
        Apply Element 1 to facts
        Conclusion on Element 1

    Element 2
        Sub-element 2A
            Apply sub-element 2A to facts
            Conclusion on sub-element 2A
        Sub-element 2B
            Apply sub-element 2B to facts
            Conclusion on sub-element 2B
        Conclusion on Element 2

    Element 3
        Applly Element 3 to facts
        Conclusion on Element 3

    Conclusion on Rule II

As Answer 1 indicates, and as the preceding box shows, there is a standard pattern for writing about each element. If an element has several parts, or sub-elements, you simply analyze each sub-element in the same way you would analyze elements. This is illustrated by Elements 2A and 2B for Rule 2. If both are required to satisfy Element 2, you need to write about both. If either would satisfy Element 2, you should still write about both if you have time. When you have completed your discussion of all the sub-elements for an element, draw a conclusion for that element.

This pattern suggests another way of thinking about the process — as a series of directions or prompts. You start by figuring out what the issues are. After that, once you've learned the pattern, the completion of each step should direct you to the next step. When you've identified the first rule, for instance, you should prompt yourself to write it down, then to write the first element of the rule, then to write the relevant facts, then to explain how the element does or doesn't apply to the facts, and then to write a conclusion. Next you direct yourself to go on to the second element, where you repeat the process. When you have finished the last element of a rule, you prompt yourself to draw a conclusion for both that element and the rule itself. Then you direct yourself to go to the next rule.

Every time you finish a step, you should know what the next step will be. This pattern, this mental map with its self-contained directions, gives you an overall guide to writing the exam. It will save you substantial time in writing your answer. Its foundation is the issues outline you prepare before you even start writing.

EXPLAINING
YOUR ANSWER

Chapter 4 gives you a "big picture" explanation of the basic steps involved in writing your answer. A variety of more specific but important matters can come up in explaining your answer, however. This chapter explains how to start writing your answer. It also provides a detailed explanation of how to state rules or elements, and how to apply them to the facts of the problem.

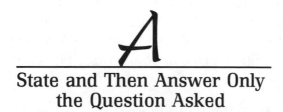

State and Then Answer Only
the Question Asked

Like the senior attorney requesting a memo addressing a particular issue, your professor wants you to answer the question being asked. You may see other issues in the problem. You may want to write an essay about the law. But you are highly unlikely to score any points for such digressions. You will score points only if you answer the question asked.

You should consider stating the question at the beginning of your answer. If you actually write the question in the exam booklet, you are more likely to answer it than if you do not. If more than one question is raised by the problem, that's another reason to state the question you are addressing before you answer it. If you state the first question, discuss your answer, then state the second question and discuss your answer, your reader is much more likely to know what you are writing about.

Professors don't ordinarily ask trick questions. If you think a question could mean two different things, pick the most obvious or straightforward meaning. If you find it necessary, explain why.

Identify and Write Each Rule That Corresponds to the Question

This is one of the most basic ways in which essay exams determine what you have learned in a course. If you get the law wrong, you may not get any credit for the answer, no matter how well argued or explained. In a legal memo, you identify these rules through research. In an exam, you should know these rules from your course work. Sometimes the problem will specifically identify the rules by name (e.g., trespass, Statute of Frauds). In such cases, issue spotting will not be necessary. But more often, you will have to figure out the rules from the question and the facts contained in the problem.

Here is additional guidance on writing the relevant rules:

1. Describe the rule accurately and precisely

For example:

GOOD: The basic measure of damages for injuries to real property is the difference between the market value of the property immediately before and immediately after the injury.

BAD: Damages to real property are measured by market value.

BAD: Courts are reluctant to uphold damages unless they are based on the difference in market value.

The first is obviously more precise. By stating the rule in such precise terms, you will make your analysis easier to understand and more complete. For example, you will know that you need to discuss the property's value both before and after the injury. If the rule is not described with reasonable precision, moreover, it will not likely get credit.

Similarly, for statutory rules, quote the relevant language if you have an open-book exam. If you have a closed-book exam, summarize it as precisely as you can. Again, if you state or summarize the rule imprecisely, you probably won't get credit. The omission of elements, exceptions, and key terms, moreover, will hurt your subsequent analysis.

Avoid shorthand descriptions of the rule or element until you have first stated it. This ensures that both you and your reader know what rule you are writing about. Do not refer to the "*Landrigan* causation test" without first describing that test in narrative terms. Similarly, do not refer to "CERCLA § 107(a)(1) liability" without first stating the rule you can find in that section.

When the rule has several elements, as it usually does, you have two choices. You can identify the rule and then, as you analyze the problem, describe its elements one by one. This choice requires you to identify the rule in some manner (i.e., by name (such as adverse possession) or by some other shorthand reference) before you start writing about each element. Or, you can state the general rule and all of the elements right away, and then repeat the elements one by one as you analyze the problem.

Either choice is fine. The first may save you time, but the second choice puts the rule in front of you as you write and may help you work through each element. A common difficulty with the second choice, however, occurs when students state all of the elements of the rule up front and then launch into a discussion without telling their reader what element they are discussing. You will not score points on an answer if your reader doesn't know what you are writing about.

Your professor may not be willing to give you credit for dicta. Sometimes, students write paragraphs saying, in effect, "The answer would be different if there was a different rule. This is the different rule, and here is how it would apply." Such paragraphs may be wasted effort, costing you time you could be writing about something for which you would get credit.

2. Explain relevant terms and concepts for the rule

Rules often include terms that require explanation or further definition. This is true of both common law and statutory rules. Stating these definitions and concepts is not simply a matter of completeness; it also provides a more solid basis for your analysis. An excerpt from Answer 1 illustrates this idea:

> Is this condition a material defect? There are two possible tests for a material defect. The objective test for a material defect is based on whether a reasonable person would attach value to the defect in deciding whether to buy . . . . The subjective test is whether the condition affects the value of the home to the particular buyer . . . .

This explanation of objective and subjective defects provides a clear understanding of both types of material defect, and thus gives you a good idea of how to frame your answer. The definition of objective defect, for instance, forces you to focus on how a reasonable person would think about buying Wallace's house. By contrast, it would be much harder to try to answer the question based solely on the idea of a material defect. Because definitions are part of the law, of course, inclusion of definitions in your answer also means your answer is likely to be more accurate and complete.

3. If two possible rules or elements could apply to the problem, use both if you have time

This may occur, for instance, when there is a majority and minority rule, and nothing in the problem limits you to one or the other. Similarly, Answer 1 discusses both the objective and subjective tests for the material defect element because both could be applied to the problem. When this happens, as Answer 1 shows, describe one of the rules or elements, apply it to the facts, and draw a conclusion. Then, if you have time, do the same for the other rule or element. If you don't have time for both, and either could apply, then be sure you discuss at least one rule or element.

On the other hand, if the question directs you to a particular rule, use that rule. Your text, for example, may discuss both the American rule and the English rule concerning a particular topic. But if the exam asks you to apply only the American rule, then limit your answer to a discussion of that rule.

For Each Element:

1. State (or restate) the element

Write the element precisely. For the nondisclosure element in the example, you could write any of these:

Was there nondisclosure?

Nondisclosure.

There was nondisclosure.

Each of these shows a way to identify the element. The latter, of course, also states a conclusion on the element. Be careful of starting your discussion with your conclusion unless you are certain you won't change it as you write. Some professors want you to state or restate the element as a conclusion before you start writing. In my experience, most do not; stating the element as a question is fine. Your professor is the final authority on this matter, of course.

2. Explain how the element applies to the facts of the problem

This part of the exam combines two components: the facts themselves, and your analysis and evaluation of the facts. Getting the issue and the rules right gets you started, but that is about all.

As explained earlier, the best exam answers include the greatest number of relevant issues, the most use of facts and policies, and the most complete and detailed explanations. An essay on the purposes of the law, the related legal rules, or the facts of the textbook cases is not a substitute for applying the law to the facts of the problem.

a. Use as many relevant facts as you can

In exams and in real life, facts give texture and complexity to problems, and have a huge effect on legal outcomes. Often, too, problems are more complicated than they seem because more than one or two facts are relevant, and because individual facts in the same problem often point toward opposing conclusions. Clients count on lawyers to understand and make sense of their factual situations.

A major difference between the best exams and the worst exams is the extent to which students use the facts of the problem. Thus, as you write and begin discussing each element, check and recheck the problem for facts that may be relevant to that element.

Consider these possibilities, which are variations on part of Answer 1 (p. 32):

ANSWER 2

Second, Wallace, the seller, created the condition. He requested that the house be used in advertising.

ANSWER 3

Second, Wallace, the seller, created the condition because he requested that the house be used in promotional brochures for the city and several tour companies, as well as in several well-known travel books. It appears that his promotional effort is the reason that a tour company bus stops in front of his house twice a month.

ANSWER 4

Wallace, the seller, created the condition.

Answer 3 is the best of the three examples because it uses more facts, and uses them more precisely. It also gives the reader an understanding of the connection between these facts and Hayakawa's concern about tourists. (There are even more facts to analyze here, as Answer 1 suggests, and as explained more fully below when we discuss counterarguments.)

Answer 2 uses fewer facts, and generalizes about the facts in a way that makes it hard to understand what really happened. Simply stating that Wallace requested that the house be used in advertising is vague about the type of advertising and makes it hard for your reader to connect that statement to Hayakawa's concern about tourists.

Answer 4, of course, is simply a conclusion, and contains no facts at all. You might think Answer 4 is too obvious to include here. Unfortunately, many law students seem to assume in their essay exams that a conclusion about facts is the same thing as a discussion of the facts. If that were true, your exam answer would only need to describe each element and draw a conclusion. That is a poor way to think about both exam writing and practicing law. In essay exams and in real life, you need to discuss all relevant facts.

b. Explain the relationship between the facts and your conclusion

As discussed in Chapter 4, simply stating the relevant legal element and facts does not automatically lead to a conclusion. Consider the objective test for material defects. You might begin your answer like this:

ANSWER 5

Third, is this condition a material defect? The objective test for a material defect is based on whether a reasonable person would attach value to the defect in deciding whether to buy. Melville's residence in the house made it more attractive for Hayakawa, and she agreed to pay a higher price for it.

If you would feel uncomfortable drawing a conclusion directly from that, your instinct is correct. You could conclude there is no defect, but that would leave Hayakawa's sense of grievance unanswered. You could conclude there is a defect, but on what basis? To analyze this particular issue, you have to figure out what a reasonable person would expect under these circumstances. You also have to connect your conclusion to Hayakawa's initial feeling that Melville's residence made the house more attractive. These explanations need to be part of your answer. Your ability to provide such explanations will play a key role in how well you do.

With these explanations, the answer (part of Answer 1) now looks like this:

ANSWER 6

Third, is this condition a material defect? The objective test for a material defect is based on whether a reasonable person would attach value to the defect in deciding whether to buy. A reasonable buyer would expect that the house would be more attractive because of Melville's residence, not less attractive. Indeed, Wallace asked — and received from Hayakawa — a higher price for the house because of Melville's previous residence. A reasonable person would buy a home for a residence, and would expect privacy in his or her home. A reasonable person would probably recognize that some tourists may want to visit a former Melville home, but the same person would not likely buy a significant tourist attraction for use as a residence. The routine presence of tourist buses and tourists, taking pictures and perhaps expecting a tour of the house interior, is not compatible with the privacy a reasonable person would expect at home.

This additional explanation and analysis is not simply lifted from the facts of the problem; it is the writer's own way of answering the question. Unless this kind of analysis and explanation is done, no conclusion to this issue will make sense. Answer 6 shows the kind of explanation and analysis that good lawyers use.

c. Use the facts accurately

Don't invent or misconstrue the facts. For example, don't say there were large numbers of tourist buses or, alternatively, that tourists virtually ignored the house. But if an important fact is unclear or missing, state your assumption about that fact as part of your explanation. For example, if the problem is silent about whether a particular event occurred, you could write that it doesn't appear from the facts that it happened.

Sometimes the problem will state something as a fact. Treat this as a fact, even if you don't agree with it. Sometimes the problem will say that someone asserted something as a fact. This is simply an assertion; it may or may not be true, and you should analyze it that way.

d. Use policies

In most textbook cases, the courts explain why the rule they are creating or applying is a good rule or why it is not appropriate to extend the rule to the factual situation before them. To the extent that those policies are relevant, use them. Don't simply repeat them, however. And never say "for policy reasons" without further explanation; that's the same as saying "because." One approach is to briefly state the way you think a rule should be interpreted or applied, and state or describe the policy that is advanced by this interpretation. Then explain *how* this policy would be furthered by your conclusion or frustrated by an opposing conclusion. Answer 1, for instance, uses the classroom discussion referred to in Chapter 1 concerning creation of the condition or defect. As a matter of fairness or equity, Answer 1 states, he should not be able to profit from nondisclosure even if he did not create the defect.

e. Use common sense

Don't limit yourself to policies in law school texts. You came into law school with certain values and experiences that shape your thinking. Don't be afraid to analyze facts in ways that reflect your own logic and reasoning. Put another way, be careful to avoid legal analysis that defies common sense.

In Answer 1, for example, the student suggests that a reasonably prudent buyer would not search travel books to find out whether a house is identified there. This responds to a potential counter-argument because the house was listed in several travel books and brochures before Hayakawa signed the contract, and it explains why this fact should not matter. But it is also based on an appeal to common sense. It is the kind of argument that a good lawyer would make to a judge or jury.

f. State your reasons accurately and precisely

You are more likely to get points on a particular element if you don't blend separate reasons together. Consider:

ANSWER 7

Fourth, is the condition peculiarly within the seller's knowledge? Yes. Wallace knew much more about the number of tourists, and what they expected, than Hayakawa did.

ANSWER 8

Fourth, is the condition peculiarly within the seller's knowledge? Yes. Both Wallace and Hayakawa knew that Melville had lived in the house. But Wallace also knew the number of tourists and their expectation of coming inside the house, which Hayakawa didn't know.

Answer 8 is more complete and precise than Answer 7 because it explains what both persons knew, and then explains what Wallace knew but Hayakawa did not know. Answer 7 compares their knowledge without being precise about what each knew, and fuses together the separate points made in Answer 8. Answer 7 also suggests, wrongly, that Hayakawa had some knowledge of the tourists.

g. Make sure your arguments are relevant to the legal rule

Compare Answer 8 with the following:

ANSWER 9

Fourth, is the condition peculiarly within the seller's knowledge? Yes. Wallace lived in the house and knew that the house attracted tourists. He should have known that Hayakawa would consider this condition to be important.

Answer 9 is not relevant to the legal rule. To say that a condition in a house is peculiarly within the seller's knowledge means that the seller is the only person who is likely to be aware of it. The answer thus requires a comparison of what Wallace knew and what Hayakawa knew. The statement that Wallace lived in the house and knew it attracted tourists helps a little. But to say that Hayakawa would consider the condition to be important is to say nothing about what Hayakawa did or did not know before she bought the house.

3. State your conclusion

Where the answer calls for you to reach a conclusion, you should write a conclusion for each element of a rule and for each rule. Although a professor may sometimes infer a conclusion from strongly stated arguments that unmistakably point to a certain conclusion without stating it, it is much safer to specifically write a conclusion. Your conclusion needs to state that something is so or that it is probably so — without waffling. Consider these phrases:

Conclusion	Not a Conclusion
probably	can argue that
probably not	may be
most likely	must prove
is liable	perhaps

It doesn't matter how you come out as long as your explanation is plausible from the facts. On some elements and facts, only one conclusion is reasonable. On other elements and facts, more than one conclusion may be reasonable. Compare Answer 6 to the following:

ANSWER 10

Third, is this condition a material defect? There are two possible tests for a material defect. The objective test is based on whether a reasonable person would attach value to the defect in deciding whether to buy. A reasonable person would recognize that some tourists may want to visit a former Melville home. Hayakawa was certainly aware that Melville had lived there. Wallace asked — and received from Hayakawa — a higher price for the house because of Melville's previous residence. Here, the tour buses come only twice a month. Because there are no organized tours of the house interior, the buses and the tourists probably do not stay outside long. Nor do the tourists have a legal right to come inside the house. They have only, at most, a license. A license is oral permission to enter or use the property of another; it is revocable at any time. To the extent Wallace's permission applied to tourists in general, it would certainly be revocable by Hayakawa as the new owner. There is no objective material defect here.

Answers 6 and 10 reach opposite conclusions, but they will not be evaluated differently because of that. For this element and these facts, either conclusion is reasonable. They will be evaluated on the basis of the legal analysis that led to the conclusion. Which analysis do you think is stronger?

The conclusion must also be internally consistent. That is, you won't get credit if you say that a necessary element of the rule is not applicable but later conclude that the rule is applicable. As discussed before, you can avoid the danger of contradictory conclusions by not stating one until you have finished your analysis. Notice that the paragraphs in Answer 1 sometimes start with conclusions and sometimes start with questions.

As important as the conclusion may be, you won't get much credit for the answer if you go straight from the issue or rule to the conclusion. Be sure to explain why the rule does or does not apply to the facts.

4. State and respond to counterarguments

Some parts of exam problems are straightforward. Only one or two facts are relevant to the element, and only one answer is plausible. For these parts of the exam, it is not usually necessary to address counterarguments.

But, as already explained, you can be sure that the most important parts of the exam—the parts where the most points are at stake—will involve counterarguments. Each fact and policy you use to answer a possible counterargument is probably worth additional points. In addition, if there is a previously unstated legal rule that would support a plausible counterargument, you should state that rule; it will help your reader understand the basis for your discussion.

Answer 1 includes several examples of counterarguments. On the first element, the writer states his or her basic explanation:

> Second, Wallace, the seller, created the condition because he requested that the house be used in promotional brochures for the city and several tour companies, and in several well-known travel books. It appears that his promotional effort is the reason that a tour company bus stops in front of his house twice a month.

This explanation is fine as far as it goes, but it doesn't include several facts that cut against the writer's conclusion. The writer thus adds:

> Wallace might say the house was already in one travel book when he moved into it. But now, because of Wallace's efforts, it is in several brochures and travel books. Wallace might also say he is not responsible for the fact that Melville lived in the house for a year. That is true, but he is responsible for the increase in tourists, which is the relevant condition. Besides, if all the other elements are met, a court might decide it doesn't matter whether he created the condition. As a matter of equity or fairness, if Wallace failed to disclose a condition of which Hayakawa could not reasonably be aware, Wallace should not profit from his behavior.

This part of the answer provides an explanation of several potentially damaging facts, and thus responds to several counterarguments. Do you see other examples of responses to counterarguments in Answer 1?

This chapter has explained how to begin writing your answer. It has also provided a lot of advice on how to write the rules, elements, or sub-elements, and how to apply them to the facts of the problem. All of this detail fits within the large-scale structure of "element-application-conclusion" described in Chapter 4.

What Exams Do Not Measure — Note 1

Essay exams do a good job of measuring a discrete set of skills, but they do not begin to measure all of the skills needed to be an effective lawyer. They do not measure your effectiveness in writing legal memos and briefs, for example. Writing an exam answer is different from writing a memo or brief because you have much less time and because you don't do research. Thus, memo and brief writing measure your ability to write and research over a more extended period. Similarly, essay exams do not measure other skills necessary to be an effective lawyer, including client counseling, oral advocacy, negotiation, alternate dispute resolution, and trial advocacy.

ORGANIZATION, SIGNPOSTING, AND WRITING STYLE

The quality of your explanation obviously matters a great deal. But if you want to be understood, your answer must also be well-written, well-organized, and signposted effectively. Because organization is so important, the first three principles in this chapter are devoted to it.

Discuss Each Rule Separately

If the answer involves failure to disclose, fraudulent misrepresentation, and trespass, for instance, complete your discussion of one before you discuss the next.

A common mistake here, particularly with statutory rules, is to write down several different rules at once and then discuss all of them at the same time. Assume, for example, that the problem (in an administrative law exam) describes an administrative agency hearing and decision, and then asks what grounds a party to the hearing may have for appealing the decision. Consider the following excerpts:

ANSWER 11

Section 555(a) of the Administrative Procedure Act (APA) states that a party "is entitled to appear in person or by or with counsel or other duly qualified representative in an agency proceeding." Section 556(d) of the APA states that a party "is entitled to conduct such cross-examination as may be required for a full and true disclosure of the facts."

[Discussion of applicability of both subsections to facts.]

ANSWER 12

Section 555(a) of the Administrative Procedure Act (APA) states that a party "is entitled to appear in person or by or with counsel or other duly qualified representative in an agency proceeding."

[Discussion of applicability of Section 555(a) to facts.]

Section 556(d) of the APA states that a party "is entitled to conduct such cross-examination as may be required for a full and true disclosure of the facts."

[Discussion of applicability of Section 556(d) to facts.]

Answer 12 is the better of the two because it discusses each rule separately. Answer 11 is hard to read, and will likely contain a confusing and incomplete discussion of how the two statutory provisions apply to the facts.

Sometimes, the order in which you discuss each rule makes it easier for you to discuss them individually. Where the factual situation in the problem involves a series of transactions or events, for instance, it is often best to discuss legal issues arising out of earlier transactions first, and then discuss legal issues arising out of later transactions. If you use chronological order, you are more likely to think about the problem clearly and keep the discussion of each issue separate. In fact, many of us think better in chronological order.

Discuss Each Element or Factor of a Rule Separately

Discuss elements and factors one at a time. Begin and complete your discussion of the first element, then the second, and so forth. Similarly, you should discuss counterarguments as part of the element to which they pertain. This helps ensure that your answer for each element is complete, and also helps you avoid repeating yourself. Thus, when you have finished discussing a particular element or factor, you should be done for good. If you mix up your discussion of separate elements, or come back to elements you have already discussed, you will likely confuse both yourself and your reader.

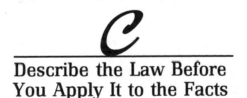

Describe the Law Before You Apply It to the Facts

If you describe the law first, the professor is much more likely to know what rule or element you are writing about and where you're going with it. You are also more likely to actually analyze the facts, rather than simply recite them, and to analyze them element by element. This is particularly important when the applicable law is a multiple-element rule that you have not yet stated.

Signpost Your Discussion

Exam scoring comes down to this: If the professor sees something worth awarding points to, you'll get the points. If he or she doesn't see it, you won't. So make it easy to read the exam; don't make your reader guess what you are writing about.

Headings are a basic way to signpost your discussion. Use headings to tell your reader what issue or rule you are discussing. You might also use headings if you are dividing your discussion in other major ways. If you are organizing your discussion by parties, for instance, you should use party names for headings. You can also use subheadings to further break down your discussion.

In addition, tell your reader what element you are discussing. Paragraphing is an essential way of signposting. You could, for example, state a multiple-element rule in one paragraph, and then use a separate paragraph for your analysis of each element. Paragraphs are useful to you in writing exams because they help you to concentrate on one rule or element at a time. They should also help your reader follow your analysis.

Another useful signposting technique is numbering the elements. Numbering, which is illustrated in Answer 1, also makes it easier for your reader to know when you are moving from one element to the next.

Write Well

Bad construction, grammar, punctuation, and spelling may make your professor less likely to give you the benefit of the doubt in scoring. Misspelled words are particularly annoying when they have been used over and over in class. Examples: "tennant," "discrimate," and "heresy," instead of tenant, discriminate, and hearsay.

Be concise. Longer answers are not necessarily better. Compare the following with Answers 7 and 8:

ANSWER 13

Is the condition peculiarly within the seller's knowledge? Yes. The condition must be one that the seller knew about. Wallace knew about it. He knew about the tourists. He had to deal with them. He even seemed to enjoy It when they came. Melville was a writer, and so is Wallace. He knew what the tourists expected. He certainly knew more than Hayakawa did.

Answer 13 is longer than the other two, but it says even less than Answer 7 (the poorer of the two earlier answers). Answer 13 is repetitive and irrelevant and does not focus on the crucial point — what Wallace knew that Hayakawa did not know. It is exceptionally hard to read such unfocused answers carefully.

Write legibly. If your professor can't even read your answer, you have reason to worry. Be careful about this when going from notes to your formal written answer, especially if your notes contain sentence fragments and code words that only you understand.

Avoid irritating errors. Some professors are bothered by errors that other professors might regard as minor. These irritations, in turn, can cost you points. Some professors, for instance, become annoyed when "she" characters are referred to as "he," and when female characters are referred by their first name while male characters are referred to by their last name. This illustrates an important point that was discussed earlier: Be sensitive to how your professor wants you to write the answer to his or her exam.

F
Don't Waste Your Time

Don't repeat yourself. After your conclusion, don't write a summary paragraph at the end. Once you've made a point, move on. Professors don't ordinarily take off points for repetitive answers, but once you start repeating yourself, they may be inclined to read a little less carefully.

What Exams Do Not Measure — Note 2

Essay exams do not measure who you are as a human being. This sounds obvious until you are in the middle of the semester putting in very long hours of study and wondering whether there is anything else in life. Everyone comes into law school with a unique personality and with his or her own individual skills, experiences, values, and aptitudes. It sometimes seems to students that law school doesn't value them as people — that they are simply "brains" to their professors, valued only to the extent they can answer questions.

It is more accurate to think of law school as adding another set of skills and experiences. It does not, and should not, replace what you started with. And, in truth, your professors don't want to do that either. In the real world of life and law practice after law school, prospective employers and clients want to hire and be with complete people. And so will your family, friends, and colleagues.

GETTING
READY

Taking exams is stressful for everyone, even those who do well. In many classes, the entire semester's grade hangs on your performance in a single final exam. But different students handle the pressure more effectively than others. These students have worked hard, but they have also worked smart.

It should go without saying that working hard is part of the law school experience. Students who work hard — who regularly attend class, who keep up with the reading, and who have prepared an outline — are more likely to do well than those who do not. But you must also work smart. That means you should know what is actually required to do well on essay exams. This book of course, is intended to help you learn that. But students who work smart also have a good attitude, learn as much as they can about what their professor wants, and practice answering hypothetical problems. These things don't eliminate anxiety from the exam process, but they do help control it.

Have a Positive Attitude

Everyone is nervous, but it helps to believe that you can do well. If you believe that, you are more likely to prepare adequately than if you don't. Even if you don't believe that you can do well, at least act like you believe it. Many students who work nervously but diligently are pleasantly surprised by their grades.

Perspective is another aspect of a positive attitude. Essay exams are only one small part of life. Students who are able to anchor their lives in something positive other than law school — family, friends, faith, or something else — are more likely to think clearly than those who don't.

Learn Your Professor's Preferences

This book provides a conceptual framework for thinking about, and answering, law school essay exams. My simple claim is that most law professors who write and grade essay exams do so in a way that is generally consistent with this framework.

This is not to say, however, that every law professor writes and grades essay exams *exactly* as described here. As in music, there are many variations on this theme. Many of these variations, in fact, have been identified in this book. Ordinarily, they are minor variations. But knowing these variations — and answering your exam based on the particular preferences of your professor — can make the difference between a good grade and a wonderful grade.

As you attend each class, listen for your professor's preferences. The conceptual framework in this book should help you know what to listen for. Your professor may say that he or she only wants you to write about issues, as opposed to each element of a rule, whether or not application of that element raises an issue. If so, you are not likely to score points on "givens." Your professor may never discuss the policy reasons that support the cases you discuss in class. If so, you are not likely to get many points for policy arguments.

If you see such differences among your professors, remember that the similarities in their approach to scoring almost certainly outweigh these differences. And be aware that judges have different preferences. Learning how to tailor your analysis for each professor is good practice for learning how to tailor your argument to a judge.

C
Practice, Practice, Practice

You should practice doing, over and over, the kind of things that are tested on the exams themselves. That is, you need to get in the regular habit of applying legal rules to new factual situations. It is not enough to read and reread your outline and text. You don't learn how to drive just by reading a booklet and observing others; you learn how to drive by driving. Soccer players don't read books on soccer technique and soccer rules before they play competitively — they practice. You learn law the same way you learn anything else that requires skill — by doing it a lot. You don't want the exam to be the first time — or even one of the first times — that you are answering hypothetical problems.

But if there is only one exam — the final exam — how do you do get the opportunity to practice? Here are some suggestions:

1. Brief the cases for class routinely, and do it yourself. That helps you with issue spotting, identification of significant facts, and evaluation of the court's analytical reasoning. It also helps you understand how policies matter and how the rules work.
2. Pay attention in class. When the professor asks you a question, you obviously need to be attentive. When the professor is calling on other students, though, try to answer the

questions in your head, and compare your answers to the answers provided by other students or your professor.

3. Treat each hypothetical question as a sample exam problem. Get comfortable answering such questions. Hypothetical problems will come up all the time in class. Hypothetical questions likely reflect your professor's current thinking about what could be tested on the exam. Some texts use a lot of problems. You can develop such problems in your study group. For most courses, too, there are other published materials containing problems you can answer. Work through them in class or on your own. As much as you can, write out your answers as if you were writing an essay exam. Then compare your answers with those the professor gives in class, the answers in a book, or the answers given by other members of your study group. Figure out what you did right and what needs to be improved.

4. If your professor gives you written problems or old exam questions, go through them with care. Try to answer them as if you were taking the exam. Then compare your answers with your professor's answers or the answers written by classmates who have done the same thing. Again, evaluate the strengths and weaknesses of your answers.

5. If you have already taken a midterm exam, or a set of exams, review your exam answers with your professor(s) to find out what you have done well and what you can improve.

Don't Think About the Exam Afterwards

This advice may be impossible to follow, but there is nothing you can do about your exam once you turn it in. Wise people have been saying for a long time that you should focus on things you can control and not worry about things you can't control. You will likely manage the period between exam time and grade announcements more sanely to the extent that you can follow this advice.

There is no definite correlation between the grade you think you will get after you've answered an essay exam and the grade you actually get. Sometimes students predict it right, but sometimes they don't. Finishing the exam with nothing more to write could be a good sign, or not. It might mean you wrote everything there is to write, or it could mean you didn't see everything you needed to answer. Finishing the exam with a lot more to say, but didn't have time to write, could also be a good or bad sign. It could mean you wrote enough to get a high grade but had more to write, or it could mean you didn't write the things you really needed to write. It is hard to know in advance, and you can drive yourself crazy trying to figure it out.

After a Property I exam several years ago, a sad-looking student apologized in advance for failing the exam. As it turned out, she received the highest grade in the class. After the Property II exam, she approached me and said that she had, for sure, flunked this one. When grades were released, she didn't do as well as she had the previous semester. She merely received an A, not the highest grade in class.

At a minimum, avoid talking to other students about what they wrote. Someone might say he wrote about something you never thought of, and this could drive you crazy. But he might have written about an incorrect issue, and your failure to write about that issue could be a good sign.

Sample Answers and Troubleshooting

This appendix contains two additional (and actual) exam problems, each of which is followed by three answers. For each problem, one of the answers is significantly better than the others. The other answers exemplify specific types of difficulties that regularly occur in exam writing. At the end of the sample answers for each problem is a brief explanation of the merits of, or weaknesses in, each answer. For each of the weaker answers, there are also suggestions for correcting or avoiding the errors it contains.

As you read the sample answers, think about how you would grade them if you were the professor, and why.

P R O B L E M

Isaac Powell owned a cottage on one acre of land in the northern part of the state. When his sister Rosalee married for the second time, he gave her a small box with a note and key inside. It was part of the pile of presents that Rosalee and Jason (the groom) opened after the wedding. The box, which was gift-wrapped, was addressed "Rosalee and Jason." The note said: "My cottage and land on Oyster Lake are yours. With all my love on your wedding— Isaac." Rosalee recognized the key as one of two keys to the cottage itself; Isaac had kept the other. Six weeks later, Isaac took a job teaching English in Ulan Bator, the capitol of Mongolia.

For the next three years, Rosalee and Jason stayed at the cottage several weeks every summer. They maintained the property, paid the local property tax as well as all utilities, and repainted the old "Oyster Lake Acre" sign on the dirt road leading to the cottage.

Isaac returned from Mongolia after three years because Rosalee was dying of cancer. They and their friends had a big party at the cottage that was both a reunion and a farewell. Several days after the party, Isaac executed a conveyance that purported to give Oyster Lake Acre to Rosalee's daughter from her first marriage, Rhonda, for the duration of Rhonda's life. Rosalee died a month later. Her will left "all my interest in real property to the National Cancer Society, and all of my personal property to Jason."

Now, in probate court, Rhonda, the National Cancer Society, Jason, and Isaac each claim to own some or all of Oyster Lake Acre. Explain how a judge would likely decide the lawful ownership of Oyster Lake Acre. Each of the four has made his/her/its best arguments.

ANSWER

Who owns Oyster Lake Acre?

GIFT

Did Isaac (the original owner for our purposes) make a valid gift of the property at the wedding? To make a gift, the donor must satisfy all of the following:

(1) Intent to make a present transfer. The note said: "My cottage and land on Oyster Lake are yours." The note said "are yours," not "will be yours," and so there is evidence of intent to make a present transfer. Isaac gave the note and key to the cottage on their wedding day, which is ordinarily an occasion for making gifts. But his keeping the other key could mean he didn't really intend to make a gift. The question of his real intent is particularly important because he later executed a conveyance of a life estate in Oyster Lake Acre to Rhonda. If he thought he had given away the property to Rosalee and Jason, he wouldn't have conveyed it to Rhonda. Six weeks after the wedding, Isaac took a job in Mongolia, and he was gone for three years. It is possible he forgot about his wedding note in that period. It is also possible he originally intended for Rosalee and Jason to use the property only while he was gone. There is insufficient evidence of intent to make a present transfer.

(2) Delivery of property to donee. According to the traditional rule, where actual manual delivery is practicable, it must be done. Actual delivery of the land and cottage is not practicable, so manual delivery is not required. When manual delivery is impossible, symbolic or constructive delivery is required.

Symbolic delivery is delivery of some object, such as a note, that is symbolic of property. Isaac here gave a note naming the Oyster Lake property, and thus effected symbolic delivery.

Constructive delivery is delivery of the means of obtaining possession and control. Isaac included a key to the cottage in the present. Because the key provided access to the interior of the cottage, and the means of using it, delivery of the key is constructive delivery of the land and cottage.

(3) Acceptance. Acceptance is presumed if the property is of value. There were no words indicating acceptance, either oral or written. But for the next three years, Rosalee and Jason stayed at the cottage several weeks every summer. Such acts do indicate acceptance. Because the first element was not met, though, Isaac did not make a valid gift.

ANSWER

Who owns Oyster Lake Acre?

GIFT

Did Isaac (the original owner for our purposes) made a valid gift of the property at the wedding? To make a gift, the donor must satisfy all of the following:

(1) Intent to make a present transfer. The note said, "My cottage and land on Oyster Lake are yours." That's a clear statement of intent. The note said "are yours," not "will be yours," and so there is evidence of intent to make a present transfer.

(2) Delivery of property to donee. According to the traditional rule, where actual manual delivery is practicable, it must be done. Actual delivery of the land and cottage is not practicable, so manual delivery is not required.

(3) Acceptance. Acceptance is presumed if the property is of value. For the next three years, Rosalee and Jason stayed at the cottage

several weeks every summer. This is acceptance, and there was probably a valid gift.

DEED

To convey an interest in land, even by gift, the grantor must also deliver a written deed to the grantee. No formal deed was delivered here, but no particular form for the deed is required. The wedding note from Isaac may be a deed if it satisfies all of the following:

(1) It must be in writing. The note was written on paper.

(2) It must be signed by the grantor. It was signed "Isaac," who is the grantor.

(3) It must identify the parties. The envelope was addressed to Rosalee and Jason, the grantees. It was signed by Isaac, the grantor.

(4) It must contain words of conveyance. Words indicating an intent to convey immediately will suffice. The note said, "My cottage and land on Oyster Lake are yours." That is enough.

(5) It must describe the property in enough detail to locate property boundaries. The note referred to "my cottage and land on Oyster Lake." That is not enough to locate the boundaries, and thus there is no valid deed.

(6) It must be delivered to the grantees. The box in which the note was located was part of the pile of presents that Jason and Rosalee opened after their wedding. There was delivery, but the deed is not valid.

EXCEPTION TO DEED REQUIREMENT

An exception to the requirement for a deed may exist, however. The Restatement rule provides one basis for that exception. The party seeking enforcement must show that, in reasonable reliance on the contract, and the continuing assent of the party against whom enforcement is sought, the party seeking enforcement has so changed its position that injustice can be avoided only by specific performance.

(1) Reasonable reliance. The Restatement rule uses the word "contract," but there is no reason to avoid applying the rule to deeds or deed-like instruments. Jason and Rosalee could reasonably rely on the authenticity of an apparent gift made "with all my love" on their wedding day.

(2) Continuing assent. Six weeks after the wedding, Isaac took a three-year job in Mongolia.

(3) The party seeking enforcement must have so changed its position that specific performance is required to avoid injustice. Specific performance here would mean awarding title in Oyster Lake Acre to Jason and whomever gets Rosalee's share. Jason and Rosalee maintained the property, paid the local property tax as well as all utilities, and repainted the old "Oyster Lake Acre" sign. They may have changed their position sufficiently to justify specific performance.

There is a valid gift. The conveyance does not satisfy the requirements for a deed but the exception applies. Isaac probably does not own the property after the wedding gift was made.

Rhonda gets nothing from the conveyance by Isaac because Isaac had nothing to convey. Jason and Rosalee received the property as tenants in common. When Rosalee died, her interest was passed by her will to the National Cancer Society. Thus, Jason and the National Cancer Society own Oyster Lake Acre as tenants in common.

ANSWER

Who owns Oyster Lake Acre?

ISAAC'S INTEREST

GIFT

Did Isaac (the original owner for our purposes) made a valid gift of the property at the wedding? To make a gift, the donor must satisfy all of the following:

(1) Intent to make a present transfer. The note said, "My cottage and land on Oyster Lake are yours." The note said "are yours," not "will

be yours," and so there is evidence of intent to make a present transfer. Isaac gave the note and key to the cottage on their wedding day, which is ordinarily an occasion for making gifts. But his keeping the other key could mean he didn't really intend to make a gift. That is particularly true because he later executed a conveyance of a life estate in Oyster Lake Acre to Rhonda. The later gift to Rhonda may show that he did not intend to give away Oyster Lake Acre at the wedding. Six weeks after the wedding, Isaac took a job in Mongolia, and he was gone for three years. It is possible he forgot about his wedding note in that period. It is also possible he originally intended for Rosalee and Jason to use the property only while he was gone. There is not likely sufficient evidence of intent to make a present transfer.

(2) Delivery of property to donee. According to the traditional rule, where actual manual delivery is practicable, it must be done. Actual delivery of the land and cottage is not practicable, so manual delivery is not required. When manual delivery is not practicable, symbolic or constructive delivery is required to effect delivery.

Symbolic delivery is delivery of some object, such as a note, that is symbolic of property. Isaac here gave a note naming the Oyster Lake property, and thus effected symbolic delivery.

Constructive delivery is delivery of the means of obtaining possession and control. Isaac included a key to the cottage in the present. Because the key provided access to the interior of the cottage, and the means of using it, delivery of the key is constructive delivery of the land and cottage.

(3) Acceptance. Acceptance is presumed if the property is of value. There were no words indicating acceptance, either oral or written. But for the next three years, Rosalee and Jason stayed at the cottage several weeks every summer. Such acts do indicate acceptance. There is no evidence that any deed to the property was recorded. That would have furnished further evidence of acceptance, but it is not needed here.

Because the first element evidently was not met, Isaac did not make a valid gift.

DEED

Even if Isaac satisfies the gift rule, he must also have delivered a written deed to the grantees. No formal deed was delivered here, but no particular form for the deed is required. The wedding note from Isaac may be a deed, if it satisfies all of the following:

(1) It must be in writing. The note was written on paper.

(2) It must be signed by grantor. It was signed "Isaac," who is the grantor. No last name is indicated, but that is not ordinarily a problem if the identity of the grantor is clear. However, the signature requirement derives from the Statute of Frauds, which is intended to prevent fraudulent or mistaken land conveyances. While there is no evidence of fraud, there is evidence of a mistake. Isaac would not likely sign only his first name on any other legal document. If he had intended to grant the land in fee simple, he would have signed his full name on a formal deed. His subsequent attempt to convey an interest in the same land to Rhonda supports that conclusion. Thus, the signature is probably not sufficient.

(3) It must identify the parties. The envelope was addressed to Rosalee and Jason, the grantees. The note was signed by Isaac, the grantor. Though no last names are identified for any of the three, their names are identified. This requirement is met.

(4) It must contain words of conveyance. Words indicating an intent to convey immediately will suffice. The note said: "My cottage and land on Oyster Lake are yours." That is enough.

(5) It must describe the property in enough detail to identify it. The note referred to "my cottage and land on Oyster Lake." There is no other description, and no reference to boundaries. But everyone appears to know which property is at issue here. An exact description of the property is not needed, and it should be possible to obtain a property description from the deed that conveyed the property to Isaac in the first place, if Isaac acquired it by deed (and not adverse possession). Also, where a deed contains a mistaken property description, it is possible to sue to reform the deed. If a mistaken property description can be reformed, an incomplete description can be made more complete. The note contains a sufficient description.

(6) It must be delivered to the grantees. The box in which the note was located was part of the pile of presents that Jason and Rosalee

opened after their wedding. Isaac either placed it on the pile or had someone else do it. Either way, Jason and Rosalee opened it. There was delivery, but the deed is probably not valid because of an inadequate signature.

EXCEPTION TO DEED REQUIREMENT

Whether the deed is valid or not, an exception to the requirement for a deed may exist. The Restatement rule is one form of that exception. The party seeking enforcement must show that, in reasonable reliance on the contract, and the continuing assent of the party against whom enforcement is sought, the party seeking enforcement has so changed its position that injustice can be avoided only by specific performance.

(1) Reasonable reliance. The Restatement rule uses "contract," but there is no reason to avoid applying the rule to deeds or deed-like instruments. Jason and Rosalee could reasonably rely on the authenticity of an apparent gift made "with all my love" on their wedding day.

(2) Continuing assent. Six weeks after the wedding, Isaac took a three-year job in Mongolia. He did nothing over a three-year period to lead Rosalee and Jason to believe that he had changed his mind. When Isaac got home, though, he executed a conveyance of a life estate in Oyster Lake Acre to Rhonda. That is inconsistent with continuing assent, but he waited three years to do it. It appears that there was continuing assent for three years, and that should be enough to satisfy the requirement.

(3) The party seeking enforcement must have so changed its position that specific performance is required to avoid injustice. Specific performance here would mean awarding title in Oyster Lake Acre to Jason and whomever gets Rosalee's share. Jason and Rosalee maintained the property, paid the local property tax as well as all utilities, and repainted the old "Oyster Lake Acre" sign. They did not make major improvements, nor were they required to pay major expenses. They only lived there several weeks each summer. They could be compensated for their relatively minor expenses to avoid any possible injustice. There is not a sufficient basis for specific performance.

Because there probably is no valid gift, the conveyance does not likely satisfy the requirements for a deed, and the exception probably does not apply, Isaac continued to be the owner in fee simple after the wedding.

CONVEYANCE TO RHONDA

When the grantor conveys a life estate to another person, without granting the remaining interest to another, the grantor leaves a reversion for himself. With his conveyance before Rosalee's death, Isaac granted a life estate to Rhonda. The grant was silent about the remaining interest. Isaac has a fee simple reversion in Oyster Lake Acre. That is his current interest.

RHONDA'S INTEREST

A conveyance to a person for the duration of that person's life creates a life estate. Isaac executed a conveyance that purported to give Oyster Lake Acre to Rhonda for the duration of Rhonda's life. Rhonda has a life estate.

JASON'S INTEREST

If there is a valid gift, and it either satisfies the requirements for a deed or the exception applies, Jason owns the property with Rosalee immediately after the wedding. What is their co-ownership interest?

Jason's best argument is that the wedding note, which was addressed to Rosalee and Jason, created a tenancy by the entirety between them. There are five requirements. First, a tenancy by the entirety is joint ownership by a married couple. Most states presume that a conveyance to a married couple creates a tenancy by the entirety even if there are no express words to that effect. If this is one of these states, a tenancy by the entirety would have been created even though there were no such words in the note.

The other four requirements are easily met. A tenancy by the entirety must be created between cotenants at the same time [in the note], by the same instrument [again, the note], with the same legal interest [there are no facts to the contrary], and the same right to possession of the whole property [again, no contrary facts]. So there would have been a tenancy by the entirety.

There is a right of survivorship with this type of tenancy. The interest of the first spouse who dies is automatically transferred at death to the surviving spouse. Thus, Jason argues, he is entitled to all of Oyster Lake Acre after Rosalee's death. Rosalee cannot convey her interest to the National Cancer Society through her will because her interest vanishes at her death.

As already explained, though, Isaac probably did not convey the property to Jason and Rosalee, and thus Jason likely has no legal interest in it.

NATIONAL CANCER SOCIETY'S INTEREST

The Society must also show that Isaac made a valid conveyance to Jason and Rosalee. The Society's best argument is that the wedding note created a tenancy in common between Jason and Rosalee. Many states presume that a conveyance to two parties, without any language referring to the type of tenancy or interest they share, creates a tenancy in common. Here, there was no such language — the note was simply addressed to Jason and Rosalee. Therefore, the Society argues that a tenancy in common was created.

A tenant in common's share is alienable and devisable; there is no right of survivorship. Rosalee left her interests in real property to the National Cancer Society. Oyster Lake Acre is included in that because it is real property and because of her tenancy in common with Jason. Thus, the Society argues, it is a tenant in common with Jason on Oyster Lake Acre. As already explained, though, Jason and Rosalee probably were never owners of Oyster Lake Acre. So the National Cancer Society likely has no legal interest in it.

Before you turn the page, which answer do you think is the best? Why?

Answer C is the best of the three answers. It answers the question that is asked, and it does so in a thorough and readable manner. Every major issue or rule is discussed separately. For each element, the element is described, relevant facts are discussed and applied, and a conclusion is stated. (Can you think of ways Answer C could be improved?)

Answer C also illustrates two useful ways to organize answers to problems that involve multiple issues and multiple parties. Most obviously, each party's ownership claim is discussed separately. There are separate sections in the answer for Isaac, Rhonda, Jason, and the National Cancer Society, and they are marked with headings to assist the reader. When the answer to the question requires you to discuss the rights or interests of multiple parties, make sure you organize your answer to include all of them.

In addition, Answer C employs a chronological form of organization, particularly concerning Isaac's interest. A chronological form of organization is especially helpful when a chain of events affects the legal rights or obligations of the parties. If you start your analysis in the middle of the chain, you are likely to confuse your reader and get it wrong to boot. Thus, the analysis starts with the note at the wedding, and discusses whether the note effectively transferred the property. After that part of the discussion is completed, issues based on later events (the conveyance to Rhonda, Rosalee's will) are discussed. As that part of the answer suggests, it is much easier to make sense out of later events when we know the legal effect of earlier events. Answer C also discusses the possible interests of Jason and the National Cancer Society, even though it is already evident they likely have no ownership of the property. The continued discussion is responsive to the question and ensures a complete answer.

Note that both of these organizational approaches are based on legal issues. The first (separate discussion of each party's interest) helps ensure that all legal issues relating to each party are discussed. Under the other, legal issues are discussed in chronological order.

Answer B makes three mistakes. Although all of the elements are included for the gift, deed, and exception issues, there is little analysis of each element. The pattern is to include one or perhaps two facts and draw a conclusion. If you carefully compare Answers B and C, you will see that Answer B reaches a different conclusion on several elements precisely because its analysis is superficial and incomplete. While the writer of Answer B may not have changed his or her conclusion because of those additional facts, he or she surely should have analyzed them.

The most basic way to correct this mistake is by including all relevant facts in your analysis, and by analyzing them as completely as time allows. As you write about each element, recheck the problem for facts relevant to that element. For each relevant fact you find, be sure to include an explanation of how it leads to your conclusion, or at least doesn't lead away from it.

The second weakness in Answer B is that it does not contain a detailed analysis of the interests of each party. The interests of Jason, Rhonda, and the National Cancer Society do not get addressed until the final paragraph of the answer, and then only in a cursory way. That is not a way to fully answer the question, or to demonstrate that you know the legal and factual basis for your conclusions.

Bare conclusions will get you very little credit on a law school essay exam. Be sure to describe the legal rule that provides the basis for your conclusion and explain how the rule applies to the facts. Also, be sure to include in your initial issues outline a list of all the parties whose interests you must address. In that way, you are more likely to allocate enough time to analyze each.

The third weakness of Answer B is that it misstates one of the elements for a valid deed. It says that a deed must accurately describe the property's boundaries. That's not the rule. The rule is that a deed must describe the property in enough detail to identify it. Answer B's analysis of this element — which focuses on property boundaries — is thus simply wrong. Many professors would award no points for that part of the answer. You can minimize such weaknesses by learning the elements cold. Doing hypothetical problems can also make you sensitive to distinctions like the one drawn here because they may involve similar factual situations. Doing hypothetical problems, in other words, can help you learn the rules better.

Answer A also made two mistakes, but they are different from those made by the writer of Answer B. The first mistake is a failure to spot all relevant issues. Answer A provides a reasonably complete answer to one issue and then stops. The writer may have believed that it was not necessary to address the deed and exception issues because he concluded there was no valid gift. That is a mistake. In the practice of law, the first issue you raise may not persuade a judge. If that is your only issue, you have a big problem. If you raise several legitimate issues, you are more likely to succeed in court.

The writer may also have simply not seen the other issues because they are harder to identify. The gift issue is pretty straightforward, but the deed and exception-to-deed issues are more difficult. Students who write about the harder issues as well as the easier ones are likely to have much higher grades than students who only see the obvious issues.

The second mistake made in Answer A is ignoring certain people's interests entirely. There is absolutely no discussion concerning Rhonda, Jason, and the National Cancer Society. In fact, there was no conclusion that answered the question asked — whose is the lawful ownership of Oyster Lake Acre? This may have occurred because the writer of Answer A did not begin the answer by restating the question. The simple act of writing the question at the beginning of the answer will reduce the likelihood of your making this mistake. In Answer B, the interests of these other parties were discussed in only a cursory way. From a grading perspective, there is likely to be little difference between an answer that ignores something and an answer that merely states a conclusion. Again, including all parties in your issues outline makes it much more likely that you will discuss their interests.

PROBLEM

75 Minutes

Mission House is a nonprofit corporation formed by a coalition of faith-based organizations to rehabilitate drug addicts. As part of its work, Mission House has begun to purchase or lease single-family homes and convert them to halfway houses for recovering addicts. To qualify for the halfway house, a person must first complete a withdrawal and prevention program to ensure that he or she is free of drugs and capable of living without them.

Last year, Mission House entered into a ten-year lease on a house in a "SF" or single family zoning district in Cambria, a city of about 75,000 people. The agreement also gives Mission House an option to purchase the property in fee simple absolute. An employee of Mission House, Jimmie Lee, has a permanent residence in the house. Three residents rent individual rooms in the house at any given time, and share dinners that Lee prepares. The residents are employed in part-time jobs around Cambria and are otherwise painting and repairing the house. No design or construction changes were needed to turn this house into a halfway house.

Cambria's zoning ordinance contains several "SF" districts in which only single-family homes are allowed. The ordinance defines a family as follows: "One or more persons occupying a single dwelling unit, provided that unless all members are related by blood, marriage or adoption, no such family shall contain more than four persons."

Recently, one of the neighbors, Frances Tyler, sued Mission House for damages, claiming that the halfway house reduces the value of her property. The complaint also truthfully alleges the following: Tyler is the original owner of the land in this particular area. Tyler had supported the constitutional amendment prohibiting the sale of alcohol. When Tyler began subdividing her property in 1935, each of the 11 deeds in the sub-divided lots contained the following: "The premises shall never be used for any purpose that is in any way related to alcohol or narcotics." The parcel now leased by Mission House was sold to Henry and Blanche Foster in fee simple absolute in 1938 with that language in the deed. In the deeds for several subsequent conveyances of the parcel since the Fosters sold it in 1954, including the deed for the 1954 conveyance, that language has been omitted. Tyler lives on the only parcel remaining from the original property that she did not convey.

No one at Mission House had actual knowledge of the deed language concerning alcohol and narcotics until the lawsuit. The residents of the Mission House property have not caused problems in the neighborhood or engaged in illegal behavior.

You represent Mission House. Does Tyler have a valid claim? Does Mission House have any valid defenses?

ANSWER

A   Does Tyler have a valid claim against Mission House based on the covenant? Does Mission House have any defenses?

In this case, Frances Tyler owned a large piece of property. She began subdividing her property in 1935. As she did, each deed in lots she carved out from her property contained this sentence: "The premises shall never be used for any purpose that is in any way related to alcohol or narcotics." Tyler was a strong supporter of the constitutional prohibition of alcohol, and did not want alcohol or drugs used on any of the property she sold. In 1938, she sold a subdivided lot to Henry and Blanche Foster in fee simple absolute. When the Fosters sold it, this language was not included in the deed. When Mission House bought it, the language was not in the deed. Tyler now lives on the only part of the original lot that she did not subdivide.

Mission House is a religious organization that seeks to rehabilitate drug addicts. It is establishing a series of halfway houses in single-family homes for recovering drug addicts. To qualify for residence in these houses, addicts must show that they have completed a withdrawal program and are capable of living without drugs.

Tyler has now sued Mission House for damages. Tyler is alleging that Mission House violates the restrictive language in the deed from her to the Fosters. Mission House has not violated this language. First of all, Mission House didn't know about it; it wasn't even in its deed. Second, Tyler's whole point was to prevent people from using her subdivided property for alcohol and drugs. Mission House has a similar objective — keeping people off drugs. Perhaps Tyler is just getting old, but her claim doesn't make sense.

Discrimination under the Fair Housing Act (FHA) must occur in one of the following ways. It can be in the terms, conditions, or privileges of sale or rental. The covenant is part of the deed, and thus is probably part of the terms or conditions of sale. To be unlawful, discrimination must also occur in the provision of services or facilities in connection with such dwelling. Here, Tyler is not providing services or facilities, but she would be preventing Mission House from providing its rehabilitation services. This requirement is met.

Is this discrimination based on handicap? A handicap is a physical or mental impairment that substantially limits one or more of a person's major life activities. Recovering alcoholics and drug addicts are considered handicapped under the FHA. These are the type of people Mission House targets. Handicap does not include current, illegal use of or addiction to a controlled substance. To qualify for the halfway house, a person must first complete a withdrawal and prevention program to ensure that he or she is free of drugs and capable of living without them. There is no evidence of current alcohol or drug use. These people are handicapped, and there is unlawful discrimination under the Fair Housing Act.

There does not appear to be a problem with the zoning ordinance. Mission House is located in a "SF" district, which means that only single-family homes are permitted there. The ordinance defines family as: "One or more persons occupying a single dwelling unit, provided that unless all members are related by blood, marriage or adoption, no such family shall contain more than four persons." Basically, the ordinance says that more than four unrelated persons cannot live together in a single-family house. Here, only four people are living in Mission House — Jimmie Lee and three recovering addicts. There is thus no violation of the zoning ordinance.

Still, is there discrimination based on handicap under the Fair Housing Act? Tyler evidently doesn't want former drug addicts in her neighborhood, reducing her property value. Former drug addicts are considered handicapped under the statute, but present drug addicts are not. The people at Mission House used to use drugs, and they have to show that they are free of drugs. They would thus be handicapped. It is precisely because of their status that Turner doesn't want them, and she is using the covenant to discriminate against them. So she violating the general rule against discrimination based on handicap.

Even if all of the requirements stated above are met, the discrimination is not unlawful under the FHA if either of two exceptions applies. In general, the first exception will apply if the following are met:

(1) The residence is any single-family house sold or rented by an owner. Tyler was the owner. She sold the lot on which Mission House is located. The Mission House lot contains a single-family house. This requirement is met.

(2) The owner doesn't own more than three such single-family houses at one time. Tyler, the owner, subdivided 11 lots, and thus owned them all once. Because this district is zoned for single-family homes, it is safe to assume that at least four of these lots are for single-family homes. There may not have been single-family houses on these

lots when she sold them, but the exception is intended to only allow small-scale discrimination. Thus, the second requirement is not met and the exception does not apply here.

The other exception applies if the following are met:

(1) The residence includes rooms or living quarters occupied by no more than four families living independently of each other. Here, one individual lives in each of three rooms, with a fourth as a permanent resident. There are four, but they do not live independently. They share meals and do various jobs around the house. They are also part of the Mission House program.

(2) The owner maintains and occupies one of such living quarters as his residence. Jimmie Lee, the permanent resident, is not the owner. He works for the owner. Neither requirement for the second exception is met, so this exception doesn't apply either.

The FHA exceptions don't apply, and thus the prohibition against discrimination provides a defense against Tyler's use of the covenant.

ANSWER

B Does Tyler have a valid claim for damages against Mission House based on the covenant? Does Mission House have any defenses?

BINDING COVENANT

Does the restrictive language concerning alcohol and drugs constitute a covenant that is binding on Mission House? A covenant is a promise to do or not to do something concerning land. A covenant is enforceable through damages, the remedy being sought here. For the covenant to be binding on subsequent owners, both the benefit and burden of the covenant must run with the land. For the burden or restriction of a covenant to run, all of the following must be met:

(1) Intent that it run. Ordinarily, this intent is expressed by language indicating that the covenant is binding on the purchaser "and his heirs and assigns." Tyler put the following language in each deed

after she began subdividing: "The premises shall never be used for any purpose that is in any way related to alcohol or narcotics." There is no reference to heirs and assigns. Tyler's statement that the land shall "never be used" probably satisfies the intent requirement. "Never" might be limited to the original grantees, the Fosters. That would explain why the covenant was not in the 1954 deed when they sold the property, and has not been in subsequent deeds. The covenant is not expressly limited to the Fosters, however. Also, intent can be inferred from whether the seller put the same language in other parcels that are being subdivided as part of a common plan. Here, Tyler included the language in every deed for the property she subdivided. There is probably intent that the covenant runs with the land.

(2) Vertical privity. Vertical privity means that the successor must succeed to the same legal estate in land as one of the original parties, not simply the same piece of land. The parcel now leased by Mission House was sold to Henry and Blanche Foster in fee simple absolute in 1938. Mission House has a ten-year lease on the house, which is a different estate in the land than fee simple ownership. This leasehold is finite in duration (ten years), unlike the fee simple. Also, the leasehold is merely possessory, and does not involve ownership. There is no vertical privity now. But Mission House has an option to buy property in fee simple absolute. If Mission House exercises the option, the vertical privity requirement will be satisfied.

(3) Horizontal privity. Horizontal privity can occur when the covenant is part of a transaction that includes transfer of benefited or burdened property. This covenant was contained in the original deed from Tyler (benefited party) to the Fosters (burdened party). There is horizontal privity.

(4) The covenant must touch and concern the land, or apply specifically to the land. The covenant states: "The premises shall never be used for any purpose that is in any way related to alcohol or narcotics." This is specific to the land, and therefore touches and concerns it.

(5) The buyer must have actual or constructive notice before purchasing it. Mission House had no actual notice of the covenant before buying the property. Constructive notice exists if there is record notice — if the covenant appeared in a recorded instrument in the buyer's chain of title. As to constructive notice, the parcel now leased by Mission House was sold to Henry and Blanche Foster in 1938 with

the covenant in the deed. When the Fosters sold the property in 1954, the language was not in the deed. It has not been in subsequent deeds. There is record notice, but it goes back to 1938. If the state has a statute that limits title searches to a 60-year period (or less) preceding the sale, this notice is probably too old to count. If the state doesn't have such a statute, the 1938 deed would likely count as constructive notice. Still, because of the lack of vertical privity, the burden does not now run with the land and the covenant is not binding on Mission House — unless Mission House exercises its option and acquires the property in fee simple.

If the benefited property has been conveyed since the original covenant, it is also necessary to show the benefit has run. Frances Tyler would be benefited by the covenant because she would prevent uses of the property relating to drug and alcohol. Tyler lives on the only parcel remaining from the original property that she did not convey. There is thus no need to show the benefit has run.

BREACH OF COVENANT

Even if the covenant is (or becomes) binding on Mission House, has Mission House breached it? A covenant should be interpreted according to the ordinary meaning of its words. These are the words: "The premises shall never be used for any purpose that is in any way related to alcohol or narcotics." This language could mean alcohol or narcotics cannot be used on the property. Mission House uses the property as a halfway house for recovering drug addicts, not to encourage or allow alcohol or drug use. But the words, "in any way," are broad enough to encompass even a halfway house.

A conveyance should also be interpreted to further the intent of the grantor. Tyler supported a constitutional amendment to prohibit alcohol. Presumably, if she supported the prohibition amendment, she would have accepted use of the property by an anti-alcohol organization. But she opposes Mission House, whose purposes seem similar to hers. It is possible to say that her purpose in the covenant was to prevent any activity that has anything to do with alcohol and narcotics. But it is also possible to say that she wants to rid the neighborhood of something she does not like, and that the covenant is simply a pretext for doing so. This argument is supported by her concern over allegedly reduced property values. Put differently, there is evidence that her current intent is not the same as her original intent, and it is her original intention that matters.

Covenants should not be read in a way that creates an illogical or strained construction. Reading this covenant to prohibit halfway houses is illogical because it is contrary to the original purpose. Though a close call, the covenant probably is not breached by Mission House's activities.

FAIR HOUSING ACT

Even if Mission House breached a binding covenant, the Fair Housing Act (FHA) may provide a defense. The defense would be available if the covenant violates the FHA.

Under Section 3604(f)(2) of the FHA, it is generally unlawful to discriminate against any person in the terms, conditions, or privileges of sale or rental of a dwelling, or in the provision of services or facilities in connection with such dwelling, because of a handicap of a person residing or intending to reside in that dwelling. To be unlawful, discrimination must meet several requirements.

The discrimination must be based, first, on a refusal to make a reasonable accommodation in rules, policies, practices, or services. A broad reading of the covenant would prohibit use of the premises for any purpose that is any related to alcohol or narcotics. That is a refusal, but is it reasonable? Reasonable accommodation means changing a generally applicable rule to make its burden less onerous on handicapped persons. Thus, reasonable accommodation here would probably permit the use of property by handicapped persons under at least some circumstances — e.g., if they were not disruptive, or if they kept up the appearance of the property. There are no complaints from the neighbors about illegal or disruptive behavior by Mission House residents or about the appearance of the property. This is refusal to make a reasonable accommodation.

Second, the refusal must concern such accommodations as may be necessary to afford handicapped persons equal opportunity to use and enjoy the dwelling. Without some accommodation, these people will not be able to live there, or anyplace like it. The requirement is satisfied.

Third, discrimination must occur in one of the following ways. It can be in the terms, conditions, or privileges of sale or rental. The covenant is part of the original deed, and thus is part of the terms or conditions of Tyler's original sale of the lot. Discrimination may also occur in the provision of services or facilities in connection with such dwelling. Here, Tyler is not providing services or facilities, but she would be preventing Mission House from providing its rehabilitation services. Either way, this requirement is met.

Fourth, the people against whom discrimination occurs must be handicapped. A handicap is a physical or mental impairment that substantially limits one or more of such person's major life activities. Recovering alcoholics and drug addicts are considered handicapped under the FHA. These are the type of people Mission House targets. Handicap does not include current, illegal use of or addiction to a controlled substance. To qualify for the halfway house, a person must first complete a withdrawal and prevention program to ensure that he or she is free of drugs and capable of living without them. There is no evidence of current alcohol or drug use, and so the exclusion for current substance abusers is inapplicable.

Finally, the discrimination must occur because of the handicap. By invoking the covenant, and claiming that it is directed at anything related to alcohol or drugs, Tyler is saying in effect that the covenant prevents recovering addicts from living in the house. Their status is precisely the basis for the discrimination. This discrimination is contrary to the statute.

EXCEPTIONS TO FAIR HOUSING ACT

Even if all of the requirements stated above are met, the discrimination is not unlawful under the FHA if either of two exceptions applies. In general, the first will apply if the following are met:

(1) The residence is any single-family house sold or rented by an owner. Tyler was the owner. She sold the lot on which Mission House is located. The Mission House lot contains a single-family house, and has been leased/rented by its owner. This requirement is met.

(2) The owner doesn't own more than three such single-family houses at one time, and does not own any interest in more than three such single-family homes. Tyler, the owner, subdivided and evidently sold 11 lots, and thus owned them all once. Because this district is zoned for single-family homes, it seems safe to assume that at least four of these lots are for single-family homes. She only owns one home now, it appears, and so the exception could be said to apply. But if it does, then she can enforce the covenant on

all 11 lots, including, but not limited to, the one on which Mission House is now located. Her ability to enforce the covenant against halfway houses is a kind of partial ownership in each of the 11 other properties. Under the statute, she doesn't need to own the homes in fee simple; any ownership interest will do. Plus, the statutory exception is intended to permit discrimination on only a small scale. Finally, there is no evidence in the problem concerning ownership of other homes by the current owner of Mission House, and so, presumably, this is not an issue. Thus, the exception probably does not apply here.

The other exception applies if the following are met:

(1) The residence includes rooms or living quarters occupied by no more than four families living independently of each other. Here, one individual lives in each of three rooms, with a fourth as a permanent resident. There are four, but they do not live independently. They share meals and do various jobs around the house. They are also part of the Mission House program.

(2) The owner maintains and occupies one of such living quarters as his residence. Jimmie Lee, the permanent resident, is not the owner. He works for the owner. Because neither requirement is met, this exception doesn't apply either.

The FHA exceptions don't apply, and thus the prohibition against discrimination provides a defense against Tyler's use of the covenant.

ANSWER

C   Does Tyler have a valid claim against Mission House? Does Mission House have any defenses?

BREACH OF EQUITABLE SERVITUDE

Does the restrictive language concerning alcohol and drugs constitute an equitable servitude that is binding on Mission House? An equitable servitude is a promise to do or not do something concerning land. An equitable servitude is enforceable through injunctive relief. For the equitable servitude to be binding on subsequent owners, the burden of the servitude must run with the land.

For the burden or restriction of an equitable servitude to run, there must be the following:

(1) Intent that it run. Ordinarily, this intent is expressed by language indicating that the covenant is binding on the purchaser "and his heirs and assigns." Tyler put this in each deed after she began subdividing: "The premises shall never be used for any purpose that is in any way related to alcohol or narcotics." There is no reference to heirs and assigns. Tyler's statement that the land shall "never be used" probably satisfies the intent requirement. "Never" might be limited to the original grantees, the Fosters. That would explain why the covenant was not in the 1954 deed when they sold the property, and has not been in subsequent deeds. The covenant is not expressly limited to the Fosters, however. Also, intent can be inferred from whether the seller put the same language in other parcels that are being subdivided as part of a common plan. Here, Tyler included the language in every deed for the property she subdivided. There is probably intent that the covenant runs with the land.

(2) The servitude must touch and concern the land, or apply specifically to the land. The covenant states: "The premises shall never be used for any purpose that is in any way related to alcohol or narcotics." This is specific to the land, and therefore touches and concerns it.

(3) The buyer must have actual or constructive notice before purchasing it. Mission House had no actual notice of the covenant

before buying the property. Constructive notice exists if there is record notice — if the covenant appeared in a recorded instrument in the buyer's chain of title. As to constructive notice, the parcel now leased by Mission House was sold to Henry and Blanche Foster in 1938 with the covenant in the deed. When the Fosters sold the property in 1954, the language was not in the deed. It has not been in subsequent deeds. There is record notice, but it goes back to 1938. If the state has a statute that limits title searches to a 60-year period (or less) preceding the sale, this notice is probably too old to count. If the state doesn't have such a statute, the 1938 deed would likely count as constructive notice. Without such a statute, the burden of the servitude runs with the land.

If the benefited property has been conveyed since the original covenant, it is also necessary to show that the benefit has run. Frances Tyler would be benefited by the covenant because she would prevent uses of the property relating to drug and alcohol. Tyler lives on the only parcel remaining from the original property that she did not convey. There is thus no need to show the benefit has run. Because the burden of the servitude runs with the land, Mission House is bound by the language in the original deed.

FAIR HOUSING ACT

Although Mission House breached a binding covenant, the Fair Housing Act (FHA) may provide a defense. The defense would be available if the covenant violates the FHA.

Under Sec. 3604(f)(2) of the FHA, it is generally unlawful to discriminate against any person in the terms, conditions, or privileges of sale or rental of a dwelling, or in the provision of services or facilities in connection with such dwelling, because of a handicap of a person residing or intending to reside in that dwelling.

Discriminate means refusal to make reasonable accommodations in rules, policies, practices, or services to any person when such accommodations may be necessary to afford such person equal opportunity to use and enjoy the dwelling.

Unlawful discrimination under this provision may occur in one of two ways. It can be in the terms, conditions, or privileges of sale or rental.

Discrimination may also occur in the provision of services or facilities in connection with such dwelling.

Is the discrimination because of a handicap of a person residing in or intending to reside in that dwelling after it is sold, rented, or made available? A handicap is a physical or mental impairment that substantially limits one or more of such person's major life activities. Recovering alcoholics and drug addicts are considered handicapped under the FHA. Handicap does not include current, illegal use of or addiction to a controlled substance.

Here, Tyler seeks to apply the language from the original deed to prevent Mission House from operating a halfway house on the property. The people using the house are considered handicapped under the FHA. She is not making a reasonable accommodation. She is plainly discriminating against them because of who they are. Her violation of the FHA provides a defense to her lawsuit.

Before you turn the page, which of the three answers is best? Why?

Answer B is the best answer. It discusses each issue fully, and discusses each element separately and completely. The Fair Housing Act issue in Answer B also provides an example of statutory analysis. Statutes are often harder to analyze because, unlike many common law rules, they don't come with a numbered list of elements. As a result, you may have to divide statutory rules into elements on your own.

Answer B also uses a number of policy arguments. It makes a distinction between the grantor's original and current intent, and suggests that honoring the current intent of the grantor would likely be likely be inconsistent with the grantor's original purpose. It also argues for a narrow construction of the Fair Housing Act exceptions because they are intended to allow only small-scale discrimination. (Can you think of ways to strengthen Answer B?)

Answer C makes four serious errors. First, the equitable servitude issue is not within the call of the question. Tyler sued for damages. The only remedy available for breach of an equitable servitude is an injunction. Real covenants, by contrast, provide a basis for damages. This student wrote about the wrong issue because he or she didn't read the question carefully or because he or she didn't know the difference between equitable servitudes and covenants. Either way, this student may not get any credit for this part of the answer.

You can correct or avoid this shortfall by being absolutely sure, going into the exam, that you know the difference between rules, particularly between closely related or similar sounding rules. In this case, many of the elements of real covenants and equitable servitudes are the same, although there are fewer requirements or elements for an equitable servitude. When you see such rules, be sure you understand how and why they differ. Train yourself, as you study, to ask questions about the material, including questions about such rules.

You can also prevent such difficulties by reading the problem carefully. The lawsuit in this case is for damages. If you pay attention to that fact, you will know that equitable servitudes are not within the call of the question. If you read the problem closely, you will also see the reference to damages as a clue that one of the issues may concern real covenants. This is simply a variation of the idea that you should think before you write.

Second, there is no discussion whatsoever in Answer C about whether the halfway house violates the restrictive language. By showing that the language constitutes a covenant or even an equitable servitude, the writer shows that the language imposes a limitation on Mission House. But it is quite another thing to show that this language actually prevents operation of the halfway house.

You can avoid this type of error by identifying in your issues outline all of the major items you must cover to answer the question. Here, in addition to deciding whether there is a real covenant, you must also decide whether the restrictive language prohibits the halfway house. Where several major points need to be covered, it is good to identify all of them in your issues outline.

Third, on the Fair Housing Act issue, Answer C provides four consecutive paragraphs describing the statutory rules without once applying the rules to the facts of the case. Essentially, this student wrote a long passage from his or her memory or outline, perhaps thinking that stating the rules is good enough. Then, in a final paragraph, Answer C contains some conclusions on several elements of the statutory rule. There is no element-by-element analysis, and very little analysis overall. This is not a good way to show your professor your ability to apply the law to the facts.

You can correct or avoid such faults by dividing statutory rules into elements, and by analyzing the statute element by element. When there is a high likelihood that the statute will be tested on the exam, you may want to break the rule into elements in your outline.

Finally, there is no analysis whatsoever of the exceptions to the Fair Housing Act. Whenever you apply a rule, especially a statutory rule, you must always be alert to the possibility that an exception applies.

Answer A makes at least five significant errors, three on the Fair Housing Act alone, and two on other issues. With respect to the covenant issue, Answer A contains no description whatsoever of the law. It simply restates the facts as if it were telling a story, and then discusses the deed language as if there is no other law to apply. Retelling the story makes your reader aware that you have read it, but that is about all. Being a lawyer means knowing and applying the law. The first step to correcting this type of error is recognizing that the professor is trying to see how well you can apply the law, not how well you can retell the story. The second step is being sure, prior to the exam that you know the rules well enough to state and apply them. (As an aside, you probably won't get points for insulting one of the parties, as in "Perhaps Tyler is just getting old . . . .")

Answer A also provides an answer to a question that wasn't asked. The issues in this problem are framed by Tyler's lawsuit, not by a claim that the zoning ordinance is being violated. It may be possible to show that a violation of the zoning ordinance could provide a basis for a lawsuit for damages. But if that connection isn't made, the answer is totally unrelated to the question being asked. The discussion of compliance with the zoning ordinance is thus simply irrelevant.

This error is somewhat like the wrong issue in Answer C, but with one difference. The wrong issue in Answer C was triggered by not reading the question carefully enough, but there were no additional facts recounted in the answer to lead the unwary astray. Here, there were "red herring" facts about the zoning ordinance included in the answer that have little if anything to do with the question or the conclusion. As previously explained, professors sometimes interject such facts into the problem to be sure you can identify the right issues. The most basic way to prevent this difficulty is to be sure, prior to writing your answer, that you understand the question. You should also be sure that the issues identified in your issues outline are responsive to the question that is asked.

Answer A makes three errors when it discusses the Fair Housing Act. The first is the disorganized way in which it discusses the issue. It includes two paragraphs on violation of the discrimination requirements, then discusses the zoning issue, then returns to the discrimination issue to repeat what was said earlier, and then discusses exceptions to the Fair Housing Act. If you felt a little confused, you can be sure that the grader may also have felt confused. Lack of organization probably explains the repetition in this answer — something that cost the writer time and yielded no additional credit.

Lack of organization is avoided by writing a good issues outline before beginning to write and then by sticking to that outline when you are actually writing the answer. The use of headings can also help prevent a disorganized essay. Answer A contains no headings at all.

The second Fair Housing Act mistake in Answer A is its failure to discuss each of the elements of unlawful discrimination under that statute. While the discussion of defenses to the statute is fairly complete, the discussion of discrimination is not. As Answer B indicates, there are five major elements for discrimination against handicapped persons under Section 3604(f)(2) of the Fair Housing Act. It is not enough to discuss only two.

This type of error is avoided by learning the elements of each rule well enough to state all of them on the exam. As suggested previously, it helps tremendously if you have already broken the rule into elements.

The third Fair Housing Act error is Answer A's failure to explain that the Act would be used as a defense to the alleged covenant. Because this problem is based on Tyler's lawsuit for damages, your reader might be wondering whether you know that the Act is relevant in this way, or if you are just writing about whatever you see with the hope that it is relevant. If you don't make the connection explicit, you may get much less credit for the answer, if you get any credit at all.

This type of mistake is corrected by being sure you understand the question before you start writing, and that you write only about issues that are relevant to its answer. Avoiding this mistake also requires that you write (and not just think of) all necessary connections between your analysis and the question itself.